Photo 5-A, Area A

A painted panel about five feet tall. The panel is painted in red and black under a shelter with an eastern facing. The body of the figure is black with a red outline. The arms and legs are in the typical posture. The red disk on the breast has a black outline which extends below enclosing a "key-hole" shaped area which is unpainted. The symbol below the figure suggests a two-headed snake or bird. However, this design, basically a trapazoid form supporting a crescent, appears in Arapaho symbolism and has several meanings as reported by Kroeber, 1902.

INDIAN

ROCK ART

IN

WYOMING

Written, illustrated and photographed

by

Mary Helen Hendry

ISBN-0-9611656-0-X

Printed by
Augstums Printing Service, Inc.
1621 South 17th Street
Lincoln, Nebraska 68502-2698

CONTENTS

ACKNOWLEDGEMENTS

I wish to express my appreciation to several groups and many individuals who assisted in so many ways with the inventory of Wyoming rock art and the study research.

The field work began in 1971, with a grant from the Wyoming Council On The Arts. In 1973, a grant was received from the National Endowment For The Arts, Washington, D.C. Some contractual assistance was received from the office of the State Archaeologist, Wyoming.

The Wyoming Archaeological Society provided guides and field assistants upon several occasions.

Helen Schuster, a former instructor in anthropology, University of Wyoming, was director of the project, 1971-72.

I particularly wish to thank George Frison, State Archaeologist and Chairman of the Department of Anthropology, University of Wyoming; George Zeimens and Danny Walker; John and Evelyn Albanese; Henry and Clara Jensen; Jim and Lucille Adams; Milford and Imogene Hanson; George and Therese Babel; Joe Bozovich; Shirley Fraker and Nona Kimball; and Scott Van Patten.

Special thanks are due Ruby Lippincott for her invaluable help in locating sites in her area and assisting on numerous trips to other parts of the state.

I am grateful to James M. Boyle, former chairman of the Art Department, University of Wyoming, and to the present chairman, James T. Forrest. Their guidance and instruction during my graduate studies were valuable preparation for the rock art study.

Lida Krans Volin and Jo Wilbert of the Natrona County Public Library were of tremendous assistance with obtaining requested research materials.

My good friends, Peggy Simson Curry and Patricia Stewart, were often along with enthusiasm and good company.

My husband, Jim, and my son, Rob, contributed to the project with their willingness to "batch" while I was off scrambling among the rocks.

February 1982
Mary Helen Hendry

ABOUT THE AUTHOR

Mary Helen Hendry received a Master of Fine Arts degree from the University of Wyoming, 1973. She was a member of the Wyoming Council On The Arts until 1973; a member of the Wyoming Bicentennial Commission until 1976; and Wyoming's representative on the American Craft Council for nine years. She recently taught three semesters of Prehistoric Art at Casper College and served six years on the Natrona County School Board.

PREFACE

This book is intended as a record of the rich contribution made by Indian artists who created their symbolic art on stone in Wyoming. Rock art is most enjoyable when it is viewed in its original outdoor setting, for the art was never intended to be collected or placed on museum walls. Rock art represents the myths and symbols of a different culture and it served that culture at that point in time as well as our art symbols serve our culture today.

In order to present a large number of photographic examples of the art, the text is brief, but it is hoped there is enough information to acquaint the reader with the interesting and significant features.

The stylistic analysis established general characteristics in the art such as typical subjects; techniques of application used; site preference; site distribution; style and distribution of style; and compositional style.

Photographs were selected as representative of site areas as identified on Map #1. A number of the photographs are printed in a manner which reverses the contrast between art and stone in order to reveal the lines of the depiction to the best advantage.

The report contains a summary of the analysis of more than two hundred Indian rock art sites recorded in Wyoming during ten years of research and fieldwork. While this is a large number of sites, others will probably be discovered.

ROCK ART

Time and weather have imperfectly erased art created by Indian peoples on isolated boulders and cliff facings, and in rock shelters and caves in Wyoming. Archaeologists call the pecked, incised and abraded designs "petroglyphs". Line drawings and painted designs are called "pictographs." A general term for all of these is rock art.

Depictions made by pecking, incising and abrading techniques were generally created on sandstone having a darker patina on the surface. The contrast between the darker patina and the original lighter colored stone below it made the designs visible. However, very little is known about the formation of patinas on stone surfaces, therefore, the degree of patina observed is not reliable for dating rock art except perhaps on a relative basis limited to an individual site.

Painted art in Wyoming is generally found in caves and rock shelters. A few examples of painted art were found on unprotected exterior surfaces and are badly weathered. Painted depictions in Wyoming rock art are usually either red or black. There are very few examples of polychrome art.

The red paint used by the Indian artists was made of crushed hematite (iron oxide) which is found in a wide range of hues, and is abundant in many areas of the state. The red pigment was pulverized and mixed with a binder such as animal fat; or the gelatinous material formed from boiling animal bones and meat; or juice from wild plants. Charcoal was used as a "pencil" for drawings and as a pigment for painting when mixed with binders such as those named above.

The patterns of the tools used to create pecked, incised and abraded art vary from site to site and even at a single site. The patterns of tools used to make pecked art are the most irregular and were probably made by whatever was at hand such as rocks, sticks, bones and pieces of antler used with a hammer stone.

The smoothness and generally well-controlled appearance of the line forming incised depictions in Wyoming rock art suggest that these were made with a knife blade or piece of metal in the Historic Period. However, technique may not represent tools available, but may indicate a tribal tradition; pecked art may have been contemporaneous with incised art.

Painted art appears to have been applied with fingers or with pieces of leather or fur. Brush marks in the art were not detected.

Stenciled art technique, appears very rarely in Wyoming. The only subject found made by this technique was the human hand. The hand prints were made by placing the hand against the stone and spraying the surface around it with a slurry made of clay and water. The spraying was probably done with the mouth of the art-maker. Human hand prints were generally made by pecking, incising, painting, or by dipping the hand in paint and pressing it against the stone.

SUBJECTS

Subjects depicted in the art are abstractions, animals, and humans.

Abstractions include circles, crescents, dots, lines, grids, chevrons, slash marks, diamonds, animal tracks, human hand and footprints and the + design. All of these appear as single and multiple elements and in various combinations, but are not numerous except for slashes. Slashes are also called "coups marks" by some rock art investigators.

Animal subjects typical in the art are deer, elk, buffalo, birds, mountain sheep, bears and horses. Turtles, antelope and mountain lions were also depicted but in very small numbers. The animals are depicted in profile except turtles and birds. Turtles are presented from their back side, and birds are presented frontally with the head turned either left or right.

In the state inventory there is one lone depiction of a rabbit. The rabbit is pecked and is in the style of rabbits painted on Mimbres mortuary pottery of the American southwest, dated about A.D. 900-1000. (See Photo 1) No painted pottery sherds or other evidence have been found in Wyoming with which to associate a date for this rock art rabbit.

POTTERY DESIGN AND ROCK ART

Frison (1978) wrote that:

"Pottery appeared in the Northwestern Plains during the Late Prehistoric Period. (A.D. 500-1700) Although present in relatively small amounts it is a valuable cultural marker. Several pottery traditions are represented. However, with one exception, the different pottery-bearing peoples were intrusive."

Photo 1, Area A

Rabbit in the style of depictions painted on Mimbres mortuary ceramic ware, A.D. 900-1000.

The exception is a style of flat-bottomed pottery generally believed to have been the production of Shoshones, but Frison noted that the . . ."original source may have been elsewhere."

The typical Late Prehistoric pottery found in Wyoming is an unpainted ware. Some examples have various surface treatments applied to the clay either in the soft or leather-hard stages during production resulting in either a partial or an over-all pattern which although representing intentional embellishment on some pottery, does not represent symbolic design resembling depictions in rock art of the study area.

Potsherds with painted geometric designs have been found in parts of southwestern Wyoming, but these were not found in association with datable materials. (Frison, op.cit.)

Depictions of horses in Wyoming rock art are valuable as indicators of its production in the Historic Period which had a beginning around A.D. 1700-1750 in the Great Plains. However, Lewis and Clark, in 1804-05, provide the earliest references to horses being used among Indian tribes roaming the territory which would become the states of Wyoming and Montana.

In Wyoming rock art, horses were depicted with all styles of human and human-like figures, but horses were not a major subject in the art whether alone or in composition with other subjects. Human and human-like depictions outnumber all other subjects in the art.

SUBSISTENCE PRACTICES AND ROCK ART

Evidence collected over years of fieldwork and research by Frison and others, indicates that hunting and gathering were the traditional means of subsistence of various groups of nomadic peoples who inhabited the Wyoming area over thousands of years. (Frison, Op.cit.; Zeimens, Walker, et al, 1977)

The hunting and gathering subsistence of the nomadic groups has inspired a theory among some rock art investigators that the purpose of rock art production was "hunting magic", meaning that the hunters created depictions of desired game animals because they believed that this would cause the animals to appear in certain locations for the kill.

Only a few human and human-like figures carry bows and arrows, spears and guns in Wyoming rock art. Figures holding bows and arrows would have been created sometime after the beginning of the Late Prehistoric Period (A.D. 500-1700) for this is the approximate time when the bow was introduced into this area.

Frison (op.cit.) noted that in Wyoming:

". . . The Late Prehistoric Period . . . is recognized by changes in projectile point types and sizes resulting from introduction of the bow and arrow" . . . and . . . "reflect a number of different cultural groups."

Gathering as part of the subsistence of nomadic Indian groups was the work of women. According to Galvan (1977) gathering meant seasonal harvesting of wild plant foods such as nuts, berries, greens, seeds, bulbs and roots. These harvested items were not subjects in the art.

Wyoming rock art-makers placed the greatest emphasis upon human-like depictions which have abstract and representational symbols on and around their bodies. Wyoming rock art is a symbolic art form. Symbolic arts of North American Indians are extensions of complex mythological and religious concepts. (The symbolic figures are discussed further under Style.)

THE SUPERNATURAL AND ROCK ART

The human-like images in Wyoming rock art may have partly symbolized supernatural spirits associated with water because the sites are characteristically located near springs, creeks, rivers, lakes, bogs and even dry gullies which occasionally run water.

The selection of certain rock facings for the art may also have been linked to symbolic concepts because the characteristic orientation of the art panels is toward the east and southeast. Panels also appear on south and southwestern facings.

The recording of rock art sites within the boundaries of the state provided hundreds of depictions for stylistic analysis. However, although there have been some archaeological excavations below cliffs covered with rock art, thus far, artifacts recovered from these sites have not provided evidence related to rock art linking it to a distant past. And, thus far, rock art depictions have not been found on the cliffs below present ground level in archaeological explorations.

BOUNDARIES

In looking for the past which contained the production of Wyoming rock art, the research was very much concerned with boundaries of various kinds. The first boundaries encountered were those of the state created in 1890, arbitrarily limiting the range of site recording.

The second group of boundaries were dictated by results of the fieldwork and site mapping which indicated areas of site concentration.

Stylistic analysis established further boundaries with distribution of different basic figural styles and compositional styles. These stylistic boundaries were researched for their archaeological and historical relationship to former and present Indian inhabitants.

Rock art depictions have been discovered in several parts of the United States, but sites are most numerous in the twelve western states of Arizona, New Mexico, Colorado, Utah, Nevada, California, Washington, Oregon, Idaho, Montana, South Dakota and Wyoming.

Montana; South Dakota, Colorado east of the Rocky Mountains; and the eastern three-quarters of Wyoming are part of the Great Plains culture area as designated by archaeologists. The Great Plains encompasses the central part of the United States between the Mississippi River and the Rocky Mountains, thence south into the northern half of Texas, and thence north into southern parts of Canada.

"Plains Indians" is a broad term applied to any of the nomadic buffalo-hunting tribes which shared a number of culture traits and once inhabited the vast Great Plains area.

LINGUISTIC DIVISIONS

Linguistic divisions of Plains Indian groups are Algonquian, Athapaskan, Caddoan, Kiowan, Siouan and Uto-Aztecan. The tribes of the Wyoming area were the Shoshones and Utes of the Uto-Aztecan linquistic group; the Blackfoot, Cheyenne and Arapaho of the Algonquian group; and various branches of the Siouan group such as the Crow and the Dakotas. These tribes entered Wyoming at different points in time and established general hunting and gathering territories.

The following is not intended to represent a comprehensive coverage of several thousand years of human presence in Wyoming, but merely offers a few archaeological and historical examples of the entry of the tribes named above.

Shoshones, or their early ancestors, are believed to have started moving into the western Wyoming area from the Great Basin well before the Historic Period. The Great Basin as an Indian culture area, contains most of Nevada and parts of Utah, California, Oregon and Idaho.

Reher (1977) described these early hunters and gatherers who entered western Wyoming from the Great Basin as follows:

"Archaic peoples, generalized hunters and gatherers in the area back 5,000 years or more ago, had a culture essentially identical to historic Great Basin Shoshonean hunters and gatherers although the Wind River Shoshone are thought by some to have expanded into the area (Wyoming) around 800 or 1000 years ago; their ancestors are still perhaps the most likely candidates for peoples traced back archaeologically five times that far."

On the eastern side of the state, in the Powder River Basin, there is evidence of bison trapping around 3,600 to 4,500 years ago. (Reher and Frison, 1980)

Archaeological evidence in the Powder River Basin also indicates a migration of prehistoric hunters and gatherers from the north around A.D. 1400.

Reher and Frison (ibid.) wrote:

"Increasing buffalo populations were probably the main factor in drawing a large migration of Athapaskan speaking people south out onto the Plains . . . others followed intermontane routes, and the Wardell buffalo kill site in the Green River Basin of Western Wyoming (ca. A.D. 600, Frison, 1973) is probably one of the very few sites documenting these migrations. Eventually most of these people were to arrive in the Southwestern United States and form the numerous Apache and Navajo."

The Crow, a member of the Siouan linguistic group, are thought by some to have split away from the Plains Village tribes along the Missouri River in the Dakotas around A.D. 1450-1700. The Crows moved west along the Yellowstone River in what is now Montana and probably began ranging south into parts of Wyoming. Frison reported radio carbon dates from sites containing Crow ceramics in eastern Wyoming.:

"The earliest dates are around 400-500 B.P. from a winter campsite at the base of the Bighorn Mountains west of Sheridan, Wyoming."

HISTORIC PERIOD

At the time of European contact, the eastern portion of Wyoming was occupied by Crow, Sioux, Cheyenne and Arapaho tribes. Journals and reports by early observers show that the Cheyenne, Arapahos and several branches of the Sioux were originally located east of the Plains and began moving west in the 18th century out of Minnesota, part of the Woodlands culture area.

Once these tribes drifted west, the Arapahos and Cheyennes began to range in the southeastern part of Wyoming and south into Colorado to the Arkansas River. (Larson, 1965)

The Crows remained in the western part of South Dakota, parts of Montana and northeastern Wyoming until later arriving branches of the Sioux tribe began pushing them farther west and along the eastern slopes of the Bighorn Mountains.

In the 1840's, as settlers and others became part of the traffic moving across the southern part of what is now Wyoming, the fighting among the Indians and their attacks upon the immigrants encouraged officials of the United States Government to call Indian tribes together in 1851, in Fort Laramie for the purpose of a peace treaty. The 1851 Peace Treaty attempted to recognize and assign to the Crows, Cheyennes, Arapahos and Sioux the lands generally occupied by them at that time, and to obtain from the Indians an agreement for safe passage across these lands for immigrants and other traffic. (See Map #2, 1851 Treaty)

The Sioux tribes were assigned lands north of the North Platte River as far west as Red Buttes (just west of present day Casper) then north to the western side of the Black Hills. (Larson, op.cit.)

The Crows were assigned the lands west of the Powder River, but were also given lands all the way west to the Wind River Mountains which were part of the territory claimed by the Shoshones who were present at the treaty meeting, but not participants in the land assignments.

The Cheyenne and Arapahos were assigned the lands of southeastern Wyoming from the North Platte to the Arkansas River in southeastern Colorado. (See Map #2, 1851, Treaty)

Later, at Fort Laramie, in 1868, the United States Government changed the assignment of Crow lands on the eastern side of the Bighorn Mountains along the Powder River and gave the area to the Sioux and Cheyenne tribes. The Crows had been under siege from the ever encroaching Sioux and Cheyennes prior to this treaty, but were finally forced to move farther west into the Bighorn Basin. (Hebard, 1930)

The continuing depredations upon the whites in spite of the 1851 Peace Treaty at Fort Laramie, and the 1868 Treaty and other efforts, have become part of the legend and history of the western frontier. There are numerous excellent references providing interesting details of the history and treaties of the period so briefly outlined above, but for the purpose of locating the territories of Indian tribes in Wyoming in relation to rock art site distribution, perhaps the foregoing outline will suffice.

STYLE, DISTRIBUTION, SITE CONCENTRATION

There are three major human figural styles in Wyoming rock art and two major compositional styles. Two of the human figural styles (Fig. 4, A and B, Basic Body Styles) are characteristic of Areas C, D, E and F, Map #1. The third human figural style (Fig. 4, D, Basic Body Styles) is characteristic of Areas A and B, Map #1.

Although the two basic body styles of Areas C, D, E and F, Map #1, have the widest distribution in the state, they represent the fewest number of sites and depictions. Areas A and B, Map #1, contain the largest number of rock art sites, or the area of site concentration. The area of site concentration is on the Wind River Indian Reservation, or in its vicinity. The reservation occupies land in both the Wind River Basin in Fremont County and in the southern Bighorn Basin on the north side of the Owl Creek Mountains in Hot Springs County.

Site distribution in Wyoming suggests that a major period of symbol-making on stone surfaces probably occurred after 1872, when the Shoshones finally settled on the Wind River Reservation designated under the Fort Bridger Treaty of 1868.

Prior to settling on the Wind River Reservation, the Shoshones were headquartered at their main home in the Green River Valley near Fort Bridger in southwestern Wyoming, but at the time of the Fort Bridger Treaty the Shoshones:

". . . Ranged from the Wind River to the North Platte throughout the Green River Valley as far south as Brown's Hole (near the southern boundary of Wyoming) and westward and southward to Bear River and the Great Salt Lake." (Hebard, op.cit.)

Members of the Northern Arapaho tribe also live on the Wind River reservation, but were "temporarily placed" there in 1877. (Larson, op.cit.) The Arapahos were enemies of the Shoshones with many bloody encounters between them, but in spite of protests from Washakie, the leader of the Shoshones, the Arapahos remained.

By court order in 1938, the Wind River reservation was divided between the Shoshones and Arapahos. The Arapahos were given permanent residence and lands on the eastern side of the reservation. The Shoshones were paid one dollar and thirty-five cents an acre for the land given the Arapahos by the U.S. Government. The price was based upon the 1878 value of the land. (Trenholm and Carly, 1964)

The treaty signed at Fort Bridger in 1868, gave the Shoshones about three million acres. An additional treaty of 1872, released an area which contained the Sweetwater Mining District, south of what is now the town of Lander. The reservation today contains about two and a half million acres.

WIND RIVER INDIAN RESERVATION ROCK ART

In the Wind River reservation area created by the 1872 treaty, rock art is distinctive from that of the Green River Valley, the former home of the Shoshones, and distinctive from the art of the larger area claimed as the former territory of the Shoshones.

Human and human-like rock art styles of the northeastern part of the Bighorn Basin (See Area A, Map #1) are similar to those characteristic in the rock art on, or near the lands of the present Crow Indian reservation in Montana, bordering Wyoming. In addition, the human figural styles of northeastern Bighorn Basin and those of the Crow Indian reservation, are both similar to the rock art styles of the Northern Cheyenne reservation and its vicinity. The Northern Cheyenne reservation borders the Crow reservation on the east.

The rock art of the Crow and Northern Cheyenne reservations is also similar to the art of Wyoming areas C, D, E and F indicated on Map #1.

In the illustration marked Fig. 4, Basic Body Styles, the characteristic body styles of Areas C, D, E and F (Map #1) which are similar to those of the Crow and Northern Cheyenne reservations in Montana, have been termed rectangular, V-necked; and circular or "shield-bearing figures." Wide distribution of rectangular and circular, or shield-bearing figures, is not confined to Wyoming and Montana. Rectangular bodied figures appear as far east as Rice County in Central Kansas. (Wedel, 1961) Mallery also reported the style in 1882-83, in eastern Nebraska, in Dakota and Thurston Counties near the Winnebago Indian reservation.

Beverly Badhorse (1979) wrote that human figures with rectangular bodies and V-necks, are typical of Northern Cheyenne rock art in Montana. Resident informants of the Northern Cheyenne reservation identified the style as religious in purpose, pertaining to the Sun Dance and about "one hundred years old."

Examples of the circular bodied or shield-bearing style figures are found as far north as Alberta, Canada and as far south as New Mexico. (Mallery, op.cit.; Fewkes, 1900)

Although distribution of style and concentration of sites indicates that a major period of creating symbolic art on stone surfaces probably occurred after 1872, on the Wind River Indian reservation, the question is were the characteristic figural style, compositional style and pecking technique invented locally, or introduced from an outside source?

SOURCE OF MAJOR REPETITIVE DESIGNS

In the section on style and compositional style to follow, the analysis indicates that a sophisticated depiction of a phallic male anthropomorphic figure about six feet tall, in Area B (See Photo 17) probably provided the "model" for the motifs and compositional styles characteristic in the art of Areas A and B, and certain compositional styles in human figural depictions in Areas C, D, E and F, Map #1.

This is not to say that the human-like figure in Photo 17, was the first rock art depiction created in Wyoming although the sophisticated image is not duplicated elsewhere in the state, nor in rock art reported in other western states. The term "sophisticated" as applied to this figure may be better understood if the reader will refer to the description of the figure accompanying Photo 17.

There was probably once a female counterpart of the Photo 17 phallic male image on an adjoining panel at the figure's left. The panel has either weathered away or been intentionally destroyed. The smaller figure at the large one's left side, was not made by the same artist and, therefore, may be a later attempt by someone to restore the large figure's missing mate.

The anthropomorphic image shown in Photo 17, was the work of a sophisticated art-maker who was probably a member of an intrusive group.

The term anthropomorph is used to describe the figure in the depiction because although it is human-like, it has eight tiny human-like figures on its breast in addition to other abstract symbols on and around its body. The elaborate, but unknown symbolism, suggests that the depiction is a supernatural personage. The eight count as symbolic design appears in other examples of Wyoming rock art.

The pecking marks which form the general outline of the figure were made by a tool held in a position which created an overlapping decorative rope-like pattern. Although pecking is the characteristic technique found in Areas A and B (See Map #1) the style of the overlapping peck marks have not been detected elsewhere.

Origin of the figure is unknown.

HISTORY OF RECORDING ROCK ART IN WYOMING

Over the years, archaeologists, both amateur and professional, have recorded rock art sites in Wyoming. Some of these recordings have been reported in various publications with comments about the general appearance and location of the art. Two important studies were made by Sowers (1940) and Gebhard (1969) who provided the most thorough photographic records of the well-known Dinwoody sites in west central Wyoming. Renaud (1936) recorded the Castle Garden sites in central Wyoming, as well as two others in Converse and Albany counties.

Probably the earliest record of rock art in Wyoming was made in 1873. Mallery, who wrote extensively about rock art around the turn of the century, noted a report made by Captain William A. Jones who made drawings of a panel discovered along the Little Popo Agie River in 1873. (See Fig. 1, after Jones and Mallery 1882-83)

A.

B.

Fig. 1, Area B

Drawings recorded in 1873, of a site along the Little Popo Agie River. (Drawing after Jones and Mallery).

Jones recording of rock art in 1873, is also mentioned in a report by Putnam, 1875, in which Putnam refers to his being present with the Jone's expedition when it camped along the Little Popo Agie River. Putnam commented that they discovered a large number of:

. . . "Hieroglyphics coarsely cut into a nearly vertical cliff of buff sandstone . . . probably not very ancient as the rock was not very hard . . . and although the site is on the Shoshone Reservation, it is frequently visited by various bands of Arapaho and Sioux while on their maurading raids." (See Fig. 2, redrawn from Putnam)

The site recorded by Jones and Putnam was recently discovered. (See designs in Photos 1-A and 1-B, as illustrated by Jones and Putnam in Fig. 2) The cliff is badly eroded, but some of the designs are still visible.

Fig. 2, Area B

Putnam's recording of the Little Popo Agie River site. (Drawing after Putnam, 1875)

Area B
1-A, designs in row A, Fig. 2, recorded in 1873.

Area B

1-B, designs in row B, Fig. 2.

Another early recording of rock art in the same general area of the Wind River Indian Reservation was made by Dr. William H. Corbusier, of the United State Army, who sent his 1882-83 recording to Mallery who included the site in his major work on rock art. (Mallery, 1886; 1893)

Corbusier's report included a drawing of the site. (See Fig. 3, after Corbusier and Mallery.) The 1882-83 drawing by Corbusier (Fig. 3) shows that the head of the figure on the left had three petal-like motifs (probably intended as feathers) and a pecked circular pattern on either side of the head.

Fig. 3, Area B

Drawing made in 1882-83, on the Wind River Reservation by Dr. William H. Corbusier, of the United States Army. (Drawing after Corbusier and Mallery).

Photo 2, is a recent (1979) photograph of the same panel. There are several differences in Corbusier's drawing and the 1979 photograph. The most obvious differences are that the figure on the left has a down-curved horned headstyle and deep slash marks on either side of the head.

Forty years ago, Sowers photographed this panel. His recording resembles that of the 1979 photograph. However, at this time, close inspection of this figure reveals that although faint, the three petal-like motifs and pecked circular patterns still exist as they did at the time of Corbusier's recording one hundred years ago. The different head motif and slash marks were added during the fifty-seven year period between 1882 and 1939. (See Photos 2-a and 2-b.)

This panel is valuable to the study because we know what a pecked figure that is at least one hundred years old looks like. The patina on the panel has nearly returned to its original color before the pecking occurred. The patina of the new headstyle seems a little lighter, but the pecking of it is deeper than that of the first design. The two slashes show darker in the photo because they were deeply gauged and pecked. As years go by, this panel may provide an example for studying the ravages of weathering and the formation of patinas.

The figure on the right side of the panel seems to have been untouched in the one hundred year period between the time it was first recorded by Corbusier and the present. The pecking technique, posture and certain motifs such as sytle of the head and multiple lines around parts of the body, are common in both Areas A and B, Map #1.

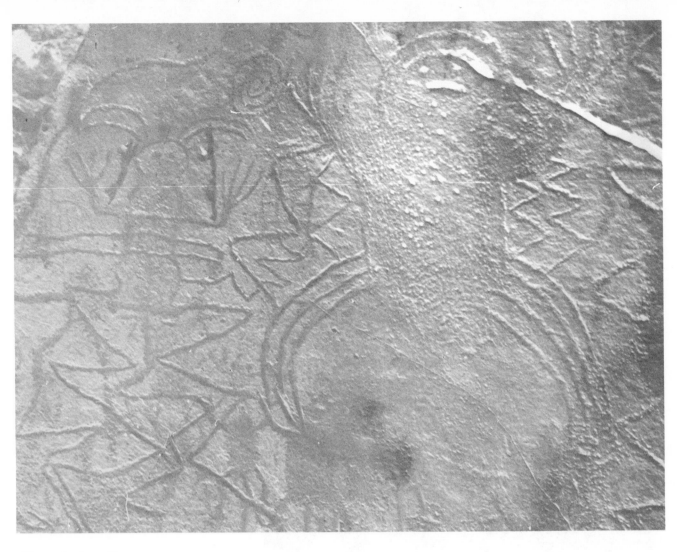

Photo 2, Area B

The same site as Corbusier's 1882-83 drawing, photographed in 1979.

Photo 2-A, Area B

Close view of the depiction on the left of the panel in Photo 2. The center "petal" or feather of the original head style can be easily detected.

Photo 2-B, Area B

The total figure at the left of the panel of Photo 2, showing the figure as it appears today, 100 years after Corbusier's drawing in 1882.

14

STYLE

The term "style" in this study refers not only to characteristic features or motifs of depictions, but also to styles of composition meaning the placement of depictions in relation to each other. The different aspects of style in the art are illustrated below, beginning with basic body styles, leg styles, head styles and followed by compositional styles.

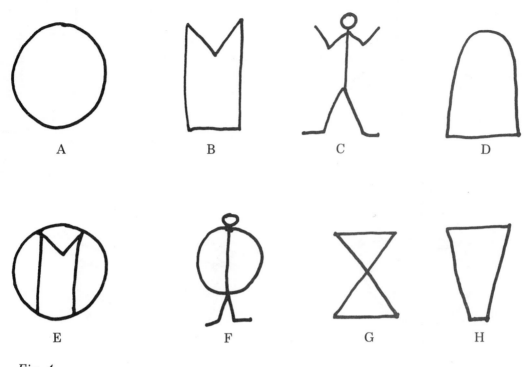

Fig. 4

Basic body styles in rock art of western states.

Rock art investigators have identified five basic body styles appearing in western states rock art. The five basic body styles have become part of rock art terminology and are illustrated in Fig. 4, A, B, C, E, F. Style "D", Fig. 4, resembles a D over on its straight side and is an additional body style found in Wyoming.

Circular styles A, E, and F, are generally lumped together and called "shield-bearing figures". Style B, rectangular body appears with straight shoulder or with V-neck, and is generally referred to as "V-necked figure". Style C is "stick figure". Styles G and H are called "Hourglass" and "Trapazoid" styles. Styles G and H are rare in Wyoming, but typical of the Fremont style of Utah.

Style A and variations E and F (Fig. 4) are called "shield-bearing figures." The interpretive term presumes a broad stylistic relationship. The presumption is probably correct, but interpretation of the purpose of the merged forms is likely more complex and related to a symbolic concept shared by the initiated of a group rather than a warrior with a shield. Fig. 5, illustrates several different expressions of the circular motif in Wyoming rock art.

The term shield-bearing figure has been part of rock art terminology used by archaeologists for more than eighty years. The earliest reference to shield-bearing figures found by this writer, is by Fewkes, 1900. Fewkes described what he called a "shield-bearing figure near Old Walpi", in Arizona. He further identified the figure as being a female with a squash blossom hair arrangement. He gave no explanation for his application of the male warrior term to a female. (See Fig. 6, redrawn from Fewkes.)

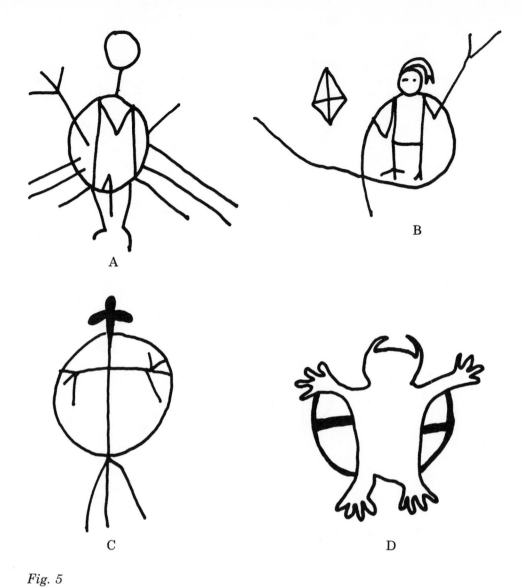

Fig. 5

Variations in the circular or "shield" motif. These figures are from four different sites.

Fig. 6

Circular bodied figure (composite) recorded by Fewkes, 1900, in Arizona. (Drawing after Fewkes)

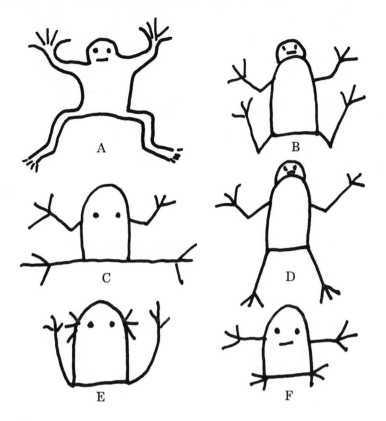

Fig. 7

Six variations in the spread leg posture.

The figures illustrated in Fig. 7, show the six variations in the spread leg posture typical of Areas A and B, Map #1. The leg positions are characteristic with basic body style D, Fig. 4, and its variations. Some of the body variations are shown in Fig. 10, Head Styles and Body Styles.

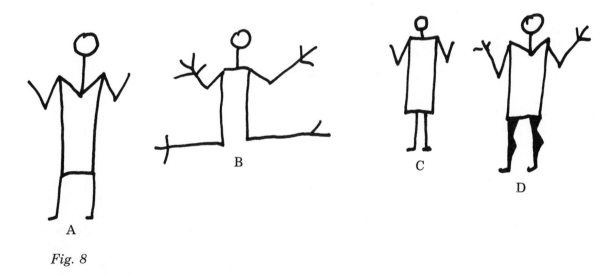

Fig. 8

Rectangular style body and typical leg posture.

Style A, having both feet pointed either left or right are typical in Areas C, D, E, and F, Map #1.

Style B, leg position is rare in Areas C, D, E and F, Map #1.

Only one example of Style C was found in the state inventory and probably is white man's art. The legs are placed as though below a garment.

Style D with thighs and calves indicated, usually appear with rectangular bodies.

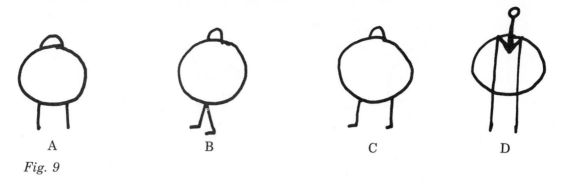

A   B   C   D

Fig. 9

Circular body and typical leg styles.

Circular bodied figures appear with a variety of leg styles shown above. Style A without feet is most common.

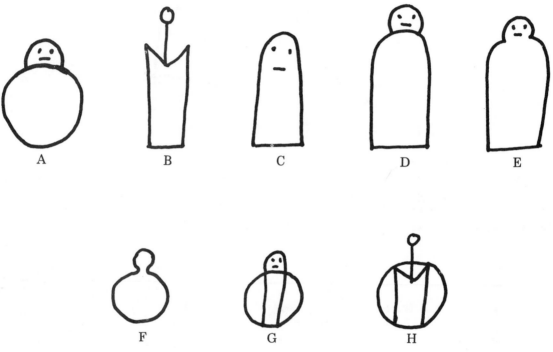

A   B   C   D   E

F   G   H

Fig. 10

Head styles and body styles.

Describing and illustrating basic head styles in Wyoming rock art necessarily involves neck and body styles. Fig. 10, shows that certain neck styles or the lack of necks, are generally related to body style. The neck styles of Fig. 10, B and H, are typical with rectangular bodied figures with V necks or straight shoulders. The neck style of these figures is exaggerated in length. Fig. 10, H, is the composite of A and B bodies with the same neck.

Fig. 10, C, D, and E are variations of the body style which resembles a D over on its straight side.

Fig. 10, C, appears to have eyes on its breast. This neck style, or lack of neck, is confined to Area B and the southern part of Area A, Map #1.

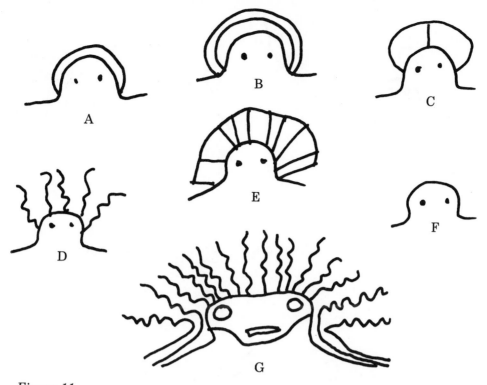

Figure 11.

Head styles, Area B and southern part of Area A.

Head styles of Fig. 11, A to F, are typical in Area B and the southern part of Area A. (See Map #1) Head style G, is the head of the sophisticated "model" composite figure of Area B. This figure is not repeated elsewhere in the state inventory.

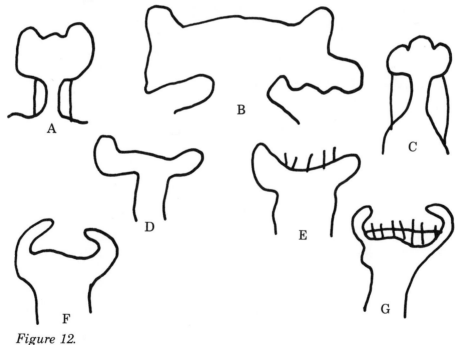

Figure 12.

Head styles of southern part of Area A.

Fig. 12, A to G, are headstyles of the southern part of Area A, Map #1. These headstyles resemble those of rock art figures of the southwestern United States where the style is called "squash blossom" hair arrangement. Styles F and G have been called "horned headdress" in Wyoming rock art. (These headstyles are solidly pecked without facial features.)

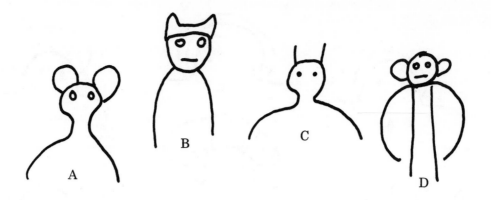

Figure 13.

Fig. 13, A to D, appear in the northeastern part of Area A. These may represent interpretations of the styles of Fig. 12.

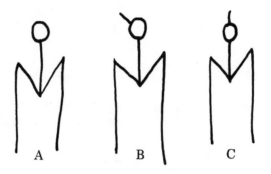

Figure 14.

Fig. 14 A, B, C, are typical of rectangular bodied figures.

COMPOSITIONAL STYLE

The common problem shared by all artists since the invention of art, is how to project ideas as forms or groups of forms through arrangement in a manner which visually "narrates" sequences of time and space for the artist and for other viewers. This "common problem" is what artists and art historians call "composition" or "design".

Over many centuries of art making, the common problem has been solved in numerous ways. One familiar method of depicting ideas about time and space on a flat surface in our contemporary culture is use of "realistic perspective". This kind of composition illustrates time and space as the human eye perceives it with objects or subjects depicted relative in size to the distance from the observer. Spatial depth is characteristic of this style of composition. The style was "invented" during the Italian Renaissance which began around A.D. 1300.

Among numerous variations in ideas compositionally expressing time and space is placement of forms in horizontal bands. One example of this style would be a Greek frieze created around 400 B.C. Another example of the same style is the Bayeux Tapestry created about A.D. 1100.

In our twentieth century experience the Greek frieze and the tapestry seem to be processionals or parades, although the first example is about ancient Greek gods and goddesses and the second example is an account of William the Conqueror's conquest of England embroidered on a tapestry that is twenty inches wide and two hundred and thirty-one feet long. Our contemporary comic strips of varying lengths are another example of the same compositional style.

Ancient Persian and Egyptian artists placed forms in horizontal bands one above the other. The bottom band represented the nearest time sequence. Those above meant later and last. Our comic strips reverse that logic and place the first time sequence across the top with later events happening as we read across and downward.

Indian art of the Northern Plains during the 1800's reflects different styles of composition. The art was created on tanned animal hides as the traditional "canvas" for paintings on items such as shields carried in warfare; buffalo robes for clothing; parfleches for storage and transportation of food; and pouches of all sizes for numerous purposes. Different purposes for the art were reflected in the compositional styles used. Hide painting compositional styles are discussed below.

WINTER COUNT COMPOSITIONAL STYLE, PLAINS INDIAN PAINTING

The few surviving specimens of Winter Count hide paintings were collected from the Sioux and Kiowa. (Ewers, 1939) Fig. 15 is an example of a Winter Count hide painting. (After Mallery, op.cit.) the Winter Count composition is a spiral arrangement of selected symbols representing a calendar of events from different "years".

Figure 15.

Winter Count compositional style using spiral arrangement of symbolic elements which form a sequence of events representing different "years" arranged in historical order. The count is told starting at the center, or with the last symbolic element on the outside edge of the circle. (Sioux artist, Drawing after Mallery, 1893)

BIOGRAPHICAL STYLE COMPOSITION IN PLAINS INDIAN PAINTING

Biographical paintings were recordings of events of bravery in warfare in an individual warrior's life. These were painted on tanned buffalo hides and were proudly worn upon special occasions by the owners of the stories.

Typical subjects painted on the hides were warriors mounted on horses. Other humans on foot and separate groupings of unmounted horses were also often included in the scene. The subjects are animated and "scattered" over the hide surface in a compositional style resembling that of twentieth century "primitive" painter, Grandma Moses, whose arrangements of subjects were an interpretation of the realistic mode of perspective of contemporary artists trained to produce it.

According to Ewers who made a study of existing specimens of Indian hide paintings in museum collections, out of 83 biographical hide paintings, the largest number, 27, were by Sioux artists. Their neighboring tribes were next with 10 from the Crow; 9 from the Kiowa; and 7 from the Cheyenne. These hides were collected in the 1800's.

Although biographical style Indian paintings were histories of the prized accomplishments of nomadic hunters, Ewers noted that game animals and hunting scenes were not depicted on the hides. Buffalo hunting was associated with the preparations and performance of the religious Sun Dance or O-Kee-Pa ceremony. Catlin's controversial account of this ceremony, as edited by Ewers (1967), provides the most detailed information about the O-Kee-Pa, and is recommended for reading in its entirety, rather than being supplied here in summary.

GEOMETRICAL STYLES OF COMPOSITION, PLAINS INDIAN PAINTING

Ewers identified five basic geometric patterns of composition painted on buffalo robes worn as clothing by Indian peoples of the Plains tribes. A style consisting of concentric circles radiating from the center with each of these circles having what appears to be feathered motifs was worn by males only. Ewers named this pattern "Feathered Circle" in his study. Women's robes were painted with patterns based upon rectangular motifs.

The Feathered Circle pattern was found only among the Sioux tribes and tribes who were known to have had close cultural contacts with them. (Ewers, op.cit.)

The Feathered Circle pattern of men's robes may have been part of the symbolism of the circular or shield-bearing style figures in rock art.

Distribution of the style shows that it is found in areas of Wyoming (D, E, and F, Map #1) considered to have been the territory of Sioux, Crow, Cheyenne and Arapaho tribes in the 1800's.

In Area C, southwestern Wyoming, the rectangular bodied and stick figural styles are more common, but circular bodied or shield-bearing figures do appear.

The spiral and geometric compositions of hide paintings do not appear in Wyoming rock art. However, a modified biographical style does appear. In rock art areas C, D, E, and F, the modified biographical style is organized as human with animal subjects. The animal subjects are buffalo, mountain sheep, deer or elk and bears. Horses are depicted alone and sometimes attached to a hand or foot of a human figure. Some human figures are "riding" horses. (See Fig. 16)

The oldest specimen of biographical style Plains Indian painting in existence is on a Mandan buffalo robe collected by Lewis and Clark in 1805, who sent it to President Jefferson. The painting is said to represent a battle fought in 1797. The specimen now belongs to the Peabody Museum of Harvard University. (Ewers, 1939)

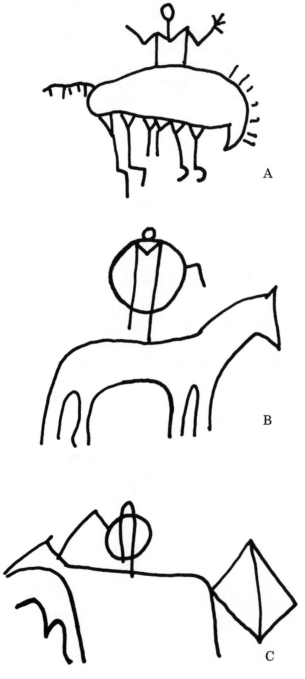

Figure 16.

Horses were introduced to Plains Indian tribes after A.D. 1700. The figural styles shown are typical of Areas C, D, E and F. (See Map #1)

Figure 17.

Long-bodied human figures A and B, appear in a biographical painting on buffalo hide of 1805, Mandan. (After Ewers, 1939) C and D, long-bodied figural styles were painted in the same biographical style on buffalo hide in 1897. Sioux artist.

Fig. 17, A and B, illustrates the style of long bodied human figures appearing on the 1805 biographical style hide painting. Fig. 17, C and D, are human figures from a buffalo robe painted in 1897, by a Sioux artist. The figural style of A, B, C and D, show a tradition of ninety-two years.

Rock art figures similar to those of the biographical style figures illustrated appear in Wyoming. Fig. 18 and 19, illustrate examples. These figures are from two different sites in Area D, Map #1. The figures are painted with red pigment. Fig. 18, A and B, were painted on the walls of a large cave. Fig. 19 A and B were found under a rock shelter formed by a fallen slab of rock against another large rock. Sand had drifted around the rock slab and had to be shoveled aside to permit entrance at one end. Remains of a fire hearth were scattered across the floor of the shelter. The length of the space under the rock is about ten feet; the width about six feet; the vertical space is about four feet, but may have been greater during occupancy. This shelter is described here in some detail because it differs from the type of rock shelter where painted art and charcoal drawings are usually found. Typical rock shelters where rock art is found are overhanging ledges of varying depths. The art was painted or drawn upon the walls and ceilings of both shelters and caves.

A

B

Figure 18.

Long-bodied human figures and V-necked retangular (long-bodied) figures painted in a cave, Area D, Map #1.

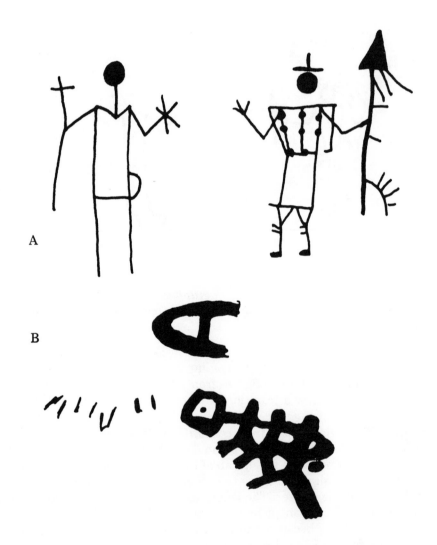

A

B

Figure 19.

Painted figures in a rock shelter formed by a fallen slab of rock. The depiction on the right of group A, has an eight count design on its breast.

Incised figures typical of Areas C, D, E and F, Map #1, are also similar to the painted styles on the Mandan and Sioux robes shown in Fig. 17. See Photo 3, which shows an incised figure with horned head style, on horseback. Incised figures outnumber painted ones, and pecked figures outnumber both incised and painted art in the state inventory.

The head style of the figure on horseback, Fig. 17, A, is called "horned headdress" by some art historians and "horned humans" by others. This head style appears with all body styles in all techniques in Wyoming rock art. (See Figs. 12, 13, 14)

Photo 3, Area C

Incised, V-necked rectangular bodied figure with horned head style on horseback. This figure is in the style of those typical in biographical style hide paintings of the 1800's, produced by Plains Indian tribes. Illustration A, in Fig. 17, is a similar example from a biographical style painting of 1805, attributed to a Mandan artist.

The figural styles of Areas C, D, E and F, Map #1, which are similar to the style of figures appearing on biographical hides painted by the Sioux and Mandans illustrated in Fig. 17, have the widest distribution, but represent the fewest number of depictions and rock art sites within the boundaries of Wyoming. These biographical hide painting figural styles in the rock art were probably adapted from hide paintings and applied to stone surfaces by tribes in the northeastern and southeastern part of Wyoming in the 1800's. Historical records from the 1800's show that the tribes which dominated the eastern part of Wyoming were Sioux, Cheyenne and Arapaho. The Crows were also in the northeastern part of the state area, but were pushed farther west and north.

COMPOSITE STYLE COMPOSITION, AREAS A AND B, MAP #1

Human-like figures of Areas A and B, often have more than one pair of arms and legs, two or more heads, or consist of large figures with smaller human-like figures on their bodies or attached to them. These composite human-like designs are probably interpretations of the design concept of the six foot anthropormorphic composite shown in Photo 17, which has eight small human-like figures in two bands of four each on its breast.

The art of Areas A and B is characteristically of pecked technique. Human-like figures tend to be larger than the incised ones of Areas C, D, E and F, previously discussed. The basic body style of Areas A and B, resembles the letter "D" turned over on its straight side.

While the composite compositional styles of Areas A and B, were expressed in an original manner typical of the two areas, the concept of merged forms used to create a symbolic narrative design has a long history in North and Central American Indian art. Such composite compositions generally express ancestral and mythological relationships; fertility and death; and religious concepts, all in one form.

COMPOSITE DESIGN

Probably the best known composite designs in North American Indian arts are the ancestral-mortuary poles (totem poles) of the Indians of the Pacific Northwest Coast. The poles have a vertical arrangement of animals combined with humans.

The practice of carving totem poles is believed to be ancient although most surviving examples are only about one hundred years old. The wet climate and the nature of the materials are credited with the destruction of older examples of the art. The earliest European explorers to report visits to permanent villages saw various kinds of carved poles at a Nootka village around 1788. (Drucker 1955)

Transformation masks of the Northwest region are an example of composite units or motifs having symbolic narrative meaning to the initiated as movable parts of the composite assemblages are manipulated. Sections are opened or closed during performance of various dances revealing two or more anthropomorphic and/or zoomorphic forms within one mask. These forms generally also have symbolic insignia upon them. This kind of composite design (intentional arrangement) is layered.

In the American southwest, several examples of composite composition (design) appear on Mimbres pottery dated A.D. 900-1000. These composites often combine two or more different kinds of animals (Fig. 20, A and D), humans with humans (Fig. 20, B) and animals with humans (Fig. 20, C and E). The illustrations of Mimbres pottery designs of Fig. 20, were selected from examples of pottery recovered during excavation of the Swart's Ruin in the Southwestern United States, and were redrawn from Cosgrove and Cosgrove, 1932.

Some of the earliest composite compositions in Indian art are found in Central America. Photo 4, is an example photographed at Tikal, showing Stela #4, dated about A.D. 386.

The complex concept of Maya symbolism expressed as composite design is defined by Willey, (1966):

"Maya gods pertain to time, to the cosmos and to agriculture. They were most often conceived of as coming in sets of four, or being in effect, four beings in one, a concept related to the four cardinal directions."

In late pre-Hispanic Mexico, the merged concepts of fertility for maize, earth, water and rain were widespread and were expressed as household idols mass produced in great quantities. A large number of these symbolized both life and death. (Nicholson, 1971)

Art of the pueblo people of the American southwest is acknowledged to have had a long tradition related to religious cermonials of fertility, crop growing, weather and harvest and with a pantheon of deities who serve as both individual and merged powers.

PEYOTE COMPOSITES

A relatively recent form of composite design created by North American Indians is composed of various symbols of the peyote religion of the Native American Church. Two of the peyote symbols are an altar in the shape of a crescent, sometimes called the new moon, and a sacred water bird.

Peyote is a small carrot-shaped cactus without spines which grows in the Southwestern United States and Mexico. The Spaniards recorded its use among the Aztecs. Some northern tribes of Mexico also used the plant in what has been described as an agricultural-hunting ritual. When buttons of the plant are eaten it produces hallucinations and sometimes vomiting. (La Barre, 1960-64; Aberle and Stewart, 1957; Slotkin, 1956; and Stenberg, 1946)

It is generally assumed by anthropologists that use of peyote among North American Indians spread from Mexico into the southern Plains around 1870, and reached some Northern Plains tribes around 1890-92, follow-

A

B

C

D

E

Figure 20.

   Composite style figures painted on Mimbres mortuary ceramic ware. Ca. A.D. 900-1000. (Drawings from photographs by Cosgrove and Cosgrove)

Photo 4

Tikal, Stela #4, A.D. 386, Guatemala. Composite design. Note the human head in the mouth of the animal.

Figure 21.

Peyote Woman. Painting on a gourd rattle of the Kiowa, recorded by Mooney, 1892. (Drawing after Mooney and Mallery)

ing the Ghost Dance period. However, peyote use was observed as early as 1850, by Indian agents in some areas. (Slotkin,ibid.)

Peyote composite-style design was described by Mooney (1892) in the human-like figure of "Mescal Woman" (Peyote Woman) painted on a Kiowa rattle used in the peyote ceremony. (See Fig. 21, after Mooney and Mallery, 1893)

Mooney's description of the composite figure is as follows:

"The lines forming the halo around the head represent the circle of devotees within the sacred lodge. The head of the figure has spots for eyes and mouth which symbolize the consecrated peyote plant which is placed upon a crescent-shaped mound within the center of the lodge. The crescent-shaped mound is represented by the downward curve of the shoulders of the female figure. Below the large crescent forming the shoulders is a smaller crescent representing the crescent of ashes formed by the fire within the crescent earth mound altar as the ceremony progresses. In the chest of the figure is a large round red disk symbolizing the fire within the crescent within the sacred lodge. The lower part of the figure's body is painted green to symbolize the eastern ocean beyond which dwells the Peyote Woman, who is the ruling spirit addressed in the ceremony. The star under her feet is the Morning Star which heralds her approach. She carries in her hand a fan of eagle feathers to shield the eyes from the glare of the fire during the ceremony. The total figure is symbolic of the sacred peyote lodge in the minds of the initiated. The rattle is to be held with the handle pointed toward the east which places the figure's feet, the open ends of the sacred crescent, and the opening to the lodge symbolically oriented toward the east." (Mooney, op.cit.)

INTERPRETATION, A BLEND OF CONCEPTS

The composite figure of Peyote Woman painted on the Kiowa rattle with its symbolism described by Mooney, is included here as an illustration of religious composite style design in Historic Period North American Indian art. The elaborate collection of symbols arranged to create a human-like figure demonstrates the difficulty in interpreting the meaning or purpose of rock art figures. We cannot say with certainty which ones may be related to peyote ritual and which ones may be associated with other religious beliefs. Composite style design in Wyoming rock art probably relates to a number of different unknown religious concepts which may be entirely Indian or partly Indian and Christian. However, there is one painted composite human-like design in the rock art which has a red disk painted on its breast, and may be an interpretation of Peyote Woman. (See Photo 5-A)

Shields carried in warfare by various tribes of Plains Indians are also religious composites. Shields were very personal expressions of supernatural powers believed to have provided protection to the individual owners. Shields were painted with symbolic designs, but were also partly collages composed of symbolic items such as feathers; animal skins; stuffed birds; parts of animals such as claws, hooves, and horns; and other amulets tied in small bundles to the shields.

Composite style design in Wyoming rock art is predominantly human-like although there are examples of animals combined with humans. (See Fig. 22)

In some rock art literature composite design such as Fig. 22, has been called 'juxtaposition and superimposition". Both terms suggest an art maker's lack of regard for what is presumed to have been previously depicted on the rock surface. The terms also presume that the component parts of a design were not contemporaneous application by one art maker, but were re-worked designs by one or more different persons at later dates. The art produced by multiple applications and by different artists might also be considered to be "palimsests" which would suggest that particular space on a rock surface may have been thought to hold special powers. However, in this study, unless it can be demonstrated that a figure has been worked on by more than one artist, the depiction is classified as composite design.

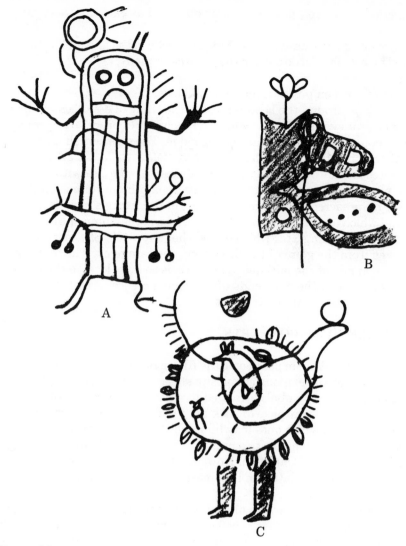

Figure 22.

Composite style design with animals and humans in Wyoming rock art.

CATEGORIES OF COMPOSITE STYLE COMPOSITION

Once composite style composition (design) was identified as a major concept in the art, attempts were made to classify variations in the style under three general categories which were arbitrarily given the descriptive titles of Host, Double and Shadow styles.

Sorting the variations of composite style did not establish separate categories of composite composition because of numerous examples of overlapping between all three categories. However, the three categories of composite composition are presented here as a means of demonstrating to the reader how to look for composite compositional concepts in Wyoming rock art.

HOST COMPOSITE DESIGN

Host design is probably the easiest composite style to identify because the depictions consist of a large figure which is "host" to one or more smaller figures on their torsos, and/or have smaller figures attached as "satellites." Examples of Host Designs are presented in Photos 5 and 6. Also see Fig. 23, as a guide to the photographs. Satellite style Host Design is shown in Photo 7.

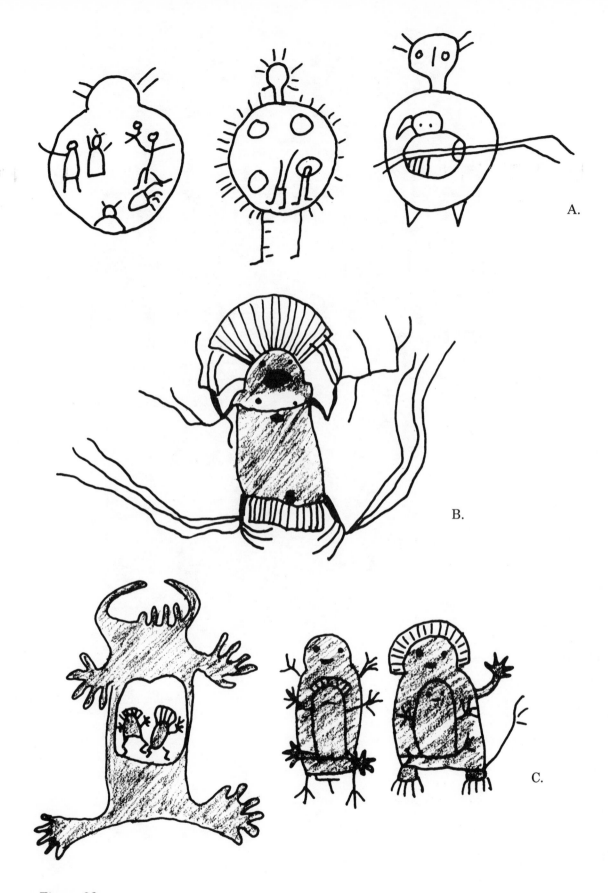

A.

B.

C.

Figure 23.

Host composite style design.

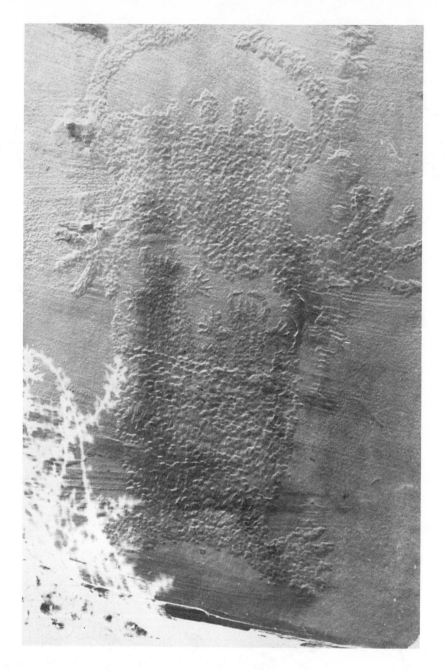

Photo 5, Area A.

Host composite design. There are two small figures on the breast of the larger one. The two small figures have the same horned head style and spread leg posture as the Host figure.

Photo 6, Area B.

Host composite design.

Photo 7, Area A.

Host satellite composite design.

DOUBLE COMPOSITE DESIGN

Double composite designs appear to have one body and two heads. One head is in the upright position and the other is inverted between spread legs of the upright figure. (See Fig. 24, and Photos 8 and 9) Double figures can generally be reversed and still "read" the same; that is, the inverted head between spread legs becomes the upright figure with raised arms when the design is turned upside down.

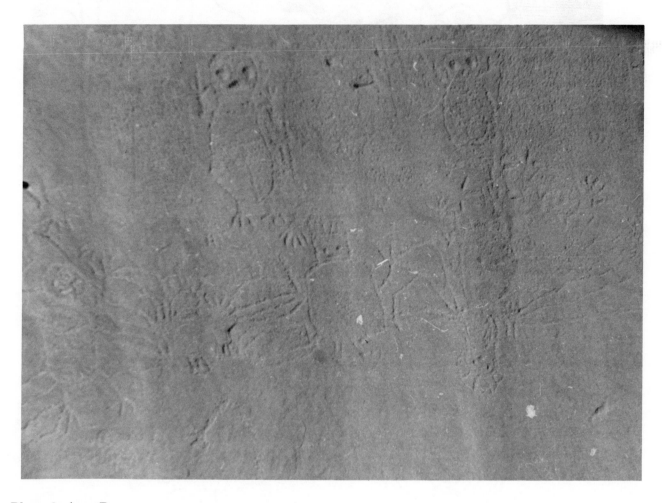

Photo 8, Area B.

Double composite design. The two lower figures at the right of the photo have heads in both the upright and the inverted positions. The upright figure at lower center has a fan-shaped head style while the inverted head below its pelvis is unadorned. The figure at lower right has an inverted head with fan-shaped headdress while the upper, or upright head is unadorned.

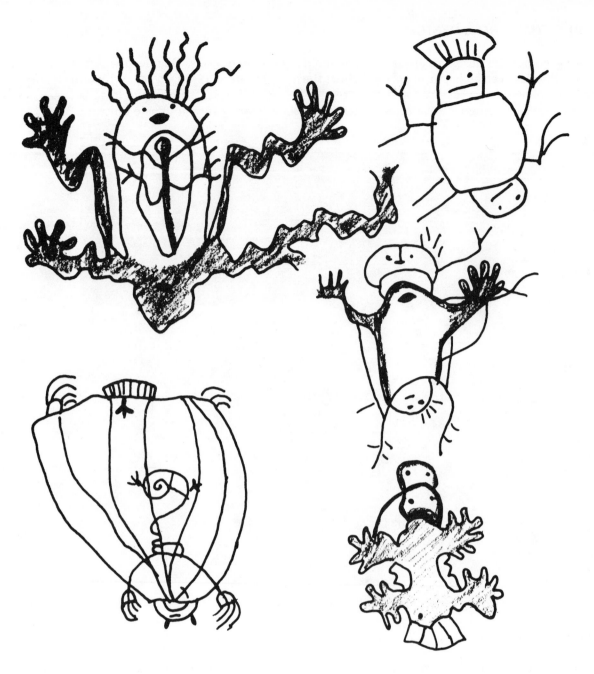

Figure 24.

Double composite style design.

Photo 9, Area A

An isolated boulder with two Double composite designs. The figure on the right has three heads, one above the other in the upright position. The inverted head between the spread legs has the fan-shaped head style.

Photo 9-A, Area A

Closer view of the Double composite on the right side of the panel on the boulder in the preceding photo.

SHADOW COMPOSITE DESIGN

Shadow composites are sometimes difficult to separate into their component parts because multiple numbers of figures are arranged as "standing behind" or enclosing other figures. (See Fig. 25, and Photos 10 and 11)

Some Shadow composite styles appear to have only one body with extra arms and legs and heads. (See Fig. 25, D) Closer inspection usually reveals additional bodies which may be identified by differences in density of pecking. (See Fig. 26, and Photo 12)

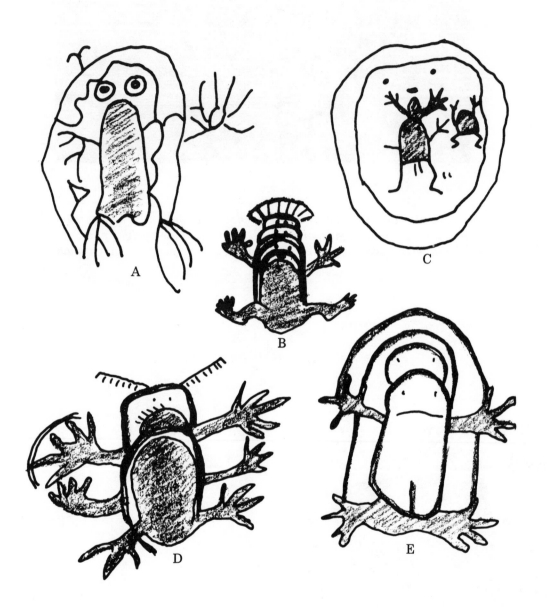

Figure 25.

Shadow composite style design.

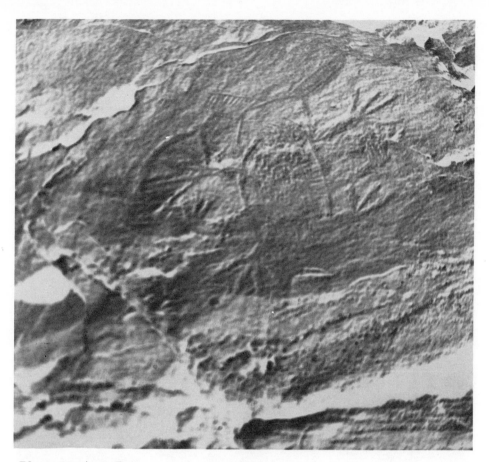

Photo 10, Area B.

Shadow composite design with six legs or arms.

Photo 11, Area B.

Shadow composite design. Three small figures appear within the large circle of another figure.

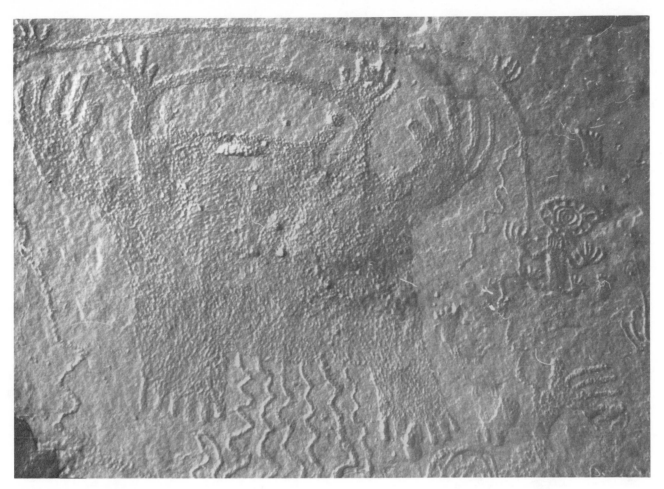

Photo 12, Area B

Shadow composite design. This composite represents at least three figures. It has a nearly hidden pecked figure in the body of the larger one which can be detected by the raised hands which appear to be "antlers" on either side of the large one's head. There are "horns" under each eye of the larger figure. The horns belong to the interior figure. The pecked line which encloses the larger solidly pecked designs also has two heads along the top, and also has one large foot attached to a leg at the figure's lower left. A drawing of this Shadow composite is shown in Fig. 26. There are small figures below and at the figure's left side.

Fig. 26

Shadow composite style design. Drawing illustrates the depiction of Photo 12.

HOST ABSTRACT COMPOSITE DESIGN

All three categories of composite design (Host, Double and Shadow) have a concept of multiple or merged human-like figural style. There are also examples where the multiple human figural composite is not totally representational in depiction, but may be an abstraction symbolizing multiple figures by using sectioned bodies (sectioned into eighths, fourths and random numbers) or with sectioned grids. See Fig. 27, and Photos 13, 14, 15 and 16.

Figure 27.

Host-abstract composite style design.

44

Photo 13, Area A.

Host-abstract composite design. Two figures with "horns" and sectioned bodies. The figure at the right has a body sectioned into eighths.

Photo 14, Area B.

Host-abstract composite design. An elaborate human-like figure in the characteristic spread-leg posture. The center portion of the body is sectioned into fourths. Above the head is a "morning star" design. A linear motif outlines the upper torso and forms a crescent above the head.

Photo 15, Area B.

    Host-abstract composite design. Pecked figure in characteristic spread-leg posture. The breast has eight sections. The head is formed by a slight curve above the breast and has the fan-shaped head style. There are smaller human-like figures above both of the large figure's feet, and an upright head at the pelvis inside the grid pattern of the lower torso.

Photo 16, Area B.

Host-abstract composite design, in the V-necked rectangular style body characteristic of Areas C, D, E, and F, (Map #1) The torso is sectioned into eighths. The figure may also have been intended to be a Double composite because there is a circle below the pelvis.

SOURCE OF THE COMPOSITE CONCEPT OF COMPOSITION

The relatively sophisticated six foot figure in Photo 17, may have provided the original source of inspiration for the largest number of human-like depictions in northwest central Wyoming and beyond. This figure is unique in Wyoming rock art and is not reported in rock art studies of other states.

The figure has numerous symbolic motifs (abstract and realistic) indicating that it is an anthropomorphic being. A large number of the embellishments of this figure, including the raised arm, spread leg posture have been borrowed and conventionalized in Wyoming rock art. A complete description of the figure follows.

Photo 17, Area B.

Host composite design. The "model" figure which provided inspiration for many of the motifs repeated in Areas A and B.

48

DESCRIPTION OF THE FIGURE IN PHOTO 17

1. The figure is an ithyphallic male approximately six feet tall. It is presented in the characteristic raised arm, spread leg squatting posture.
2. The technique of application was pecking through a light red, naturally formed patina on the stone. The design is composed of both lines and areas of solid pecking.
3. The tool used to make the pecked marks of the general outline of the body was held at an angle which created an overlapping pattern.
4. Double row of pecked outline from the base of the thumbs following the curve of the arms and shoulders. The double line is incorporated into the hair or headdress on either side of the head.
5. Triple row of pecked outline from underside of hand and following the bend of the elbow. The triple outline continues from under the arm and follows the contours of the torso, bent leg and arch over the top of the foot. The lines discontinue over the ends of the toes and over the finger tips.
6. The triple rows of outline continue on the underside of the legs and also outline the crotch and phallus.
7. Seventeen vertical lines appear below the crotch. The tops of the vertical lines are bent to the right on the figure's right, and to the figure's left.
8. There is an area of solid pecking below the phallus and a flower-like pattern among the vertical lines under the figure's left leg.
9. The hair or headdress consists of twelve wavy lines radiating from the head, plus the two lines on either side of the head from the ends of the double outline. There is a total of sixteen lines around the figure's head.
10. The face of the figure has only eyes and a mouth deeply pecked through a solidly pecked area which resembles a mask.
11. The body, legs, arms, hands and feet are solidly pecked except for the neck and two "window-like" areas across the upper breast.
12. The window-like areas contain eight small figures which are solidly pecked in two rows of four each. (See Photo 18, detail)

Photo 18, Area B.

Detail of the breast of the "model" figure in Photo 17, showing the eight tiny figures.

49

13. The eight tiny figures are in the characteristic raised arm, spread leg or squatting posture of the Host figure.
14. In the center of the breast, at the base of the throat, is an abstract symbol consisting of a solidly pecked circle surrounded by smaller circles. The lower portion of the design is badly eroded, but the spacing of the existing small circles suggests that there may have been a total of eight. (See Photo 19, detail)
15. The area of pecking on the Host figure's lower torso forms a diagonal pattern from upper left to lower right.
16. A small figure appears near the large Host figure's left knee. The figure is about thirty inches tall. It appears in the characteristic posture and may be a Double Composite, but the pattern below the pelvis is not too distinct.
17. The smaller figure just described is attached to the large Host figure by a line from the top of its head and from its right fingers, and from its knee to the Host figure's triple outline. The smaller figure is partially destroyed on its left side.
18. Above the large Host figure's left hand is part of another depictions' feet which just meet the fingers of the Host figure.
19. Traces of what may have been part of a large panel of art are found at the right of the Host figure. The stone surface has been destroyed by weather or intentionally. The panel may have once held a female counterpart of the phallic male.

Photo 19, Area B.

Detail of the breast of the "model" figure showing the circular symbol at the throat of the design.

The following list of repetitive motifs appear in the rock art at other sites. These motifs are probably interpretations of those of the "model" figure described above. The motifs of the model figure appearing elsewhere in Wyoming rock art were probably inspired directly and indirectly by the Host figure. Direct inspiration means an art maker's interpretation after viewing the model figure. Indirect inspiration means creating an interpretation of the model figure after viewing the rendering of it by another art maker's interpretation.

MAJOR MOTIFS OF HUMAN-LIKE FIGURES IN WYOMING ROCK ART

1. Pecked lines and incised lines arranged in a variety of ways appear with human-like figures. The lines may be single, double, triple or multiple. The lines appear to hang from under arms, from wrists, from legs, from crotch. Some are fastened between arms and legs. Some appear around heads, shoulders and bodies. (See Fig. 28)
2. Feet generally consist of spread toes varying in number from zero to seven.
3. Arms are depicted in raised position with bent elbows.
4. Hands generally consist of spread fingers varying in number from two to nine on one hand.
5. Spread legs, squatting posture appears in six variations. (See Fig. 7) Descriptions below.
   a. Legs spread wide apart with knees bent.
   b. Legs spread wide apart and held upward as if knee joints were reversed, or the figure were kneeling or squatting.
   c. Legs spread wide apart, held straight out from hips.
   d. Legs spread apart, held straight down from hips.
   e. Legs spread apart and curving upward from hips.
   f. Legs "missing" but figure has feet attached at the hips. Fig. 7, E, shows similar attachment of hands without arms. The absence of arms and legs may indicate that these appendages are held close to the body with only hands and feet extended.
6. Sectioned bodies
   a. Totally sectioned into eighths.
   b. Totally sectioned into fourths.
   c. Totally sectioned into random numbers.
   d. Sectioned into grid patterns or window-like areas on upper body.
7. Composite style composition.
8. Size is not conventionalized in the total state inventory, the range of sizes is from three inches to six feet among human-like figures. The largest depictions are found in Areas A and B, with one exception in Area E where three nearly life-sized figures were found at one site. (See Photos 20 and 21)

COMPOSITE STYLE COMPOSITION IN AREAS C, D, E AND F, MAP #1

The human-like figures of Areas C, D, E and F, characteristically are rectangular and circular (shield-bearing) types. The compositional style (intentional arrangement) of figures of Areas C, D, E and F, is similar to that of Plains Indian biographical paintings of the 1800's, which documented the accomplishments of warriors in battle. The four figures illustrated in Fig. 29, are examples of a design concept consisting of multiple human-like figures merged together in various combinations. Fig. 29-A, is a deeply incised human depiction with multiple arms and the circular motif. Fig. 29-B, is an incised rectangular bodied Host style composite which appears to have three heads as well as a small figure partly on its breast and partly between spread legs. Fig. 29-C, is a deeply incised rectangular style with a tiny figure upright between its legs. Fig. 29-D, is a charcoal drawing of a Double composite with an inverted head painted black.

The vertical rectangular figure in Photo 20, is an outstanding example of a Host composite design in Area E, Map #1. The figure is nearly life size and has three smaller stylized human-like figures on its breast. (See Photo 21) The three small figures are long bodied and similar to those appearing in Winter Counts painted by the Sioux of the 1800's (See Fig. 15, and Fig. 30) The three small figures also have bodies sectioned by chevrons. (They have no legs)

The large Host figure of Photo 20, a phallic male, is not in the typical raised arm, spread leg posture of Host composites in Areas A and B. The legs of the figure in Photo 20, are articulated and have thighs and calves defined. The figure is one of three large figures at the site with several smaller ones. The three large figures appear to have been created by the same artist, but have differnt motifs and embellishments. All three large figures have arrows directed at the lower portion of the legs.

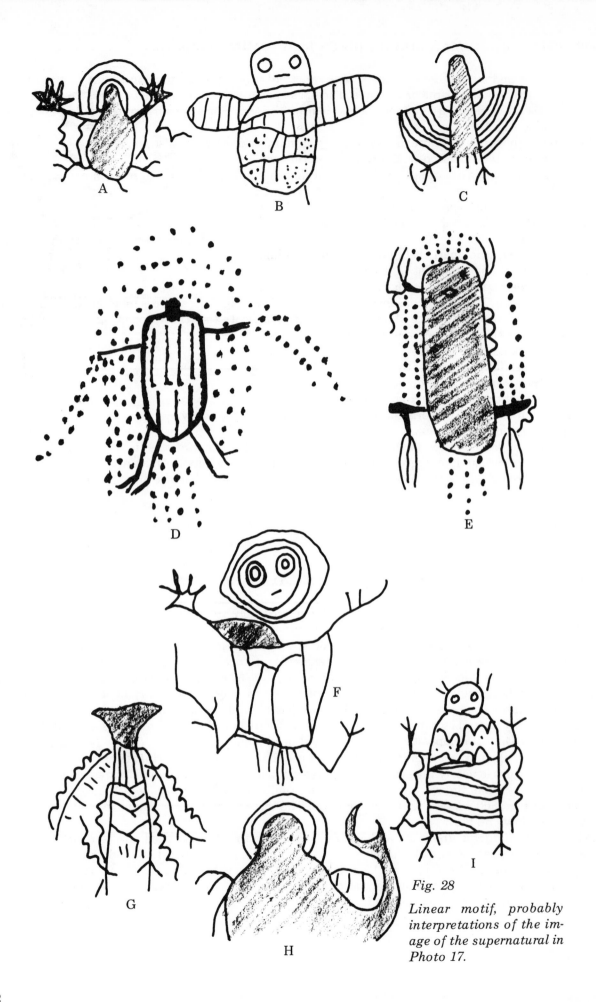

Fig. 28

Linear motif, probably interpretations of the image of the supernatural in Photo 17.

Figure 29.

Composite style composition in Areas C, D, E and F, Map #1.

Photo 20, Area E.

Two life size human figures. The figure on the right of the photo is a Host composite with three small figures on its torso. The small figures have no legs or arms, but the bodies are divided into chevrons. These three small figures are in the style of those used on a Winter Count hide painting of a Sioux Indian, Lone Dog. (See Fig. 30) There are arrows around the lower part of the legs of both large figures. The panel of art probably was made in the late Historic Period.

Photo 21, Area E.

Detail of the breast of the figure in Photo 20. The small figure at the left of the photo shows the head and body style to the best advantage.

Figure 30.

A and B, are Winter Count style human figures which also appear at some rock art sites in Wyoming. C, is a symbol which Mallery (1893) called a "rake". The symbol has eight vertical lines and appears on Winter Count hide paintings. Mallery reported that Indian informants interpreted the symbol as "death". The rake symbol appears at some rock art sites in Wyoming. It does not always have eight vertical lines. (Designs were drawn after Lone Dog and Mallery)

GHOST DANCE SYMBOLISM IN WYOMING ROCK ART

One of the last periods of rock art production in Wyoming, and probably in a number of other western states as well, was associated with the Ghost Dance Religion of 1890-92. The Ghost Dance, a blend of Christian resurrection doctrine and Indian religion, originated among the Northern Paiutes of the Walker River Indian reservation in northwestern Nevada, and spread rapidly among thirty-five different tribes throughout the western United States. (Mooney, 1896)

Symbols adopted by participants of the 1890-92 Ghost Dance were: a circle representing the sun; a horizontal crescent representing the "new" moon; the morning star in several variations based upon a + design; sacred birds which were identified as the crow, magpie and eagle; handprints; dots; slashes; fish; pipes; buffalo; turtles and the cedar or pine tree used by some tribes as a focal point for their dancing.

All of the symbols listed above appear in Wyoming rock art except fish and pipes. The sacred birds and grooved slashes were the most often repeated symbols of the Ghost Dance in Wyoming rock art, and are noted in the captions in the photographic section.

The title "Ghost Dance" was bestowed upon the religion by whites in reference to the concept of resurrection of the dead through periodic dancing. However, the "new" religion meant much more than that to the Indian people. It was an expression of hope for the return of the old way of life which had come to an end. Indian people once free to wander the land were confined to reservations.

The Northern Paiute prophet-leader of the 1890-92 Ghost Dance was Wovoka. Wovoka proclaimed that periodic performance of a certain circle dance for a duration of two years would return dead Indian ancestors to life; buffalo and other wild game would again be plentiful; and the white invaders would be exterminated. At the end of the two year dance period, Wovoka said the earth would be destroyed, renewed and returned to Indian people. The doctrine promised protection for Indians with the help of the sacred birds during destruction of the earth. The birds would carry Indians aloft to safety and return them when the earth was ready.

The Ghost Dance of 1890-92 was not unique, among Indian tribes; it was a revival of earlier religious movements with the same theme. The earlier forms of the doctrine began around 1850 in the northwest. Two of the groups were the Shakers of Puget Sound and the Dreamers along the Columbia River.

Twenty years before the Ghost Dance began on the Walker River reservation, a relative of Wovoka had started a similar religious movement there. The 1870 movement and the northwest versions spread rapidly, flourished for a time and then seemed to have faded away until 1889.

GENERAL SITE CHARACTERISTICS

1. The technique used to create the designs were pecking, incising and abrading (petroglyphs) and line drawings and paintings (pictographs). Wyoming rock art includes all techniques. Pecked designs are characteristic in northwest central Wyoming (Area A and B, See Map #1). Incised art is characteristic in Areas C, D, E, F. (See Map #1) Incised technique has the widest distribution, but represents the smallest number of sites. Pecked technique represents the largest number of sites. There are but few painted and line drawing style depictions in the total state inventory. (Area A has the most sites with painted technique).

2. Pecked and incised depictions (petroglyphs) were applied to exposed cliff and boulder surfaces. Painted depictions and drawings (pictographs) are found in protected rock shelters and caves.

3. Petroglyphs generally are found pecked or incised through a naturally formed patina on sandstone. The patina ranges in hue from light red to dark red-brown.

4. Depictions appear on east, south, southeastern and southwestern facings. Very rarely do depictions appear on north facings.

5. Depictions are usually at eye level or lower on the panels. There are a few examples of the art on high cliffs. The latter designs would have required a ladder or scaffold of some sort, or the art makers were suspended from the top of the cliff. Possibly, the art makers may have used small cliff ledges while creating the designs and then destroyed the ledges following completion of the art.

6. There are examples of intentionally destroyed depictions and partially destroyed depictions in the vicinity of the Wind River Indian reservation. Partially destroyed depictions have only heads remaining. These heads have fan-shaped headdresses. The fan-shaped headdress appears on some Double Composite style human-like figures. This style of composite has both an upright head and an inverted head between spread legs. These figures are described in more detail under the section on Composite Design.

7. Rock art sites are generally found near water. This includes creeks, springs, lakes, rivers and sometimes near the mouth of dry washes and gullies.

PHOTOGRAPHIC SECTION

The following examples of rock art are from the state-wide inventory. The photographs are divided according to site areas A, B, C, D, E and F as identified on Map #1.

Illustrations on the pages with photographs are not necessarily from the same site, but are from the same geographical area.

Area A

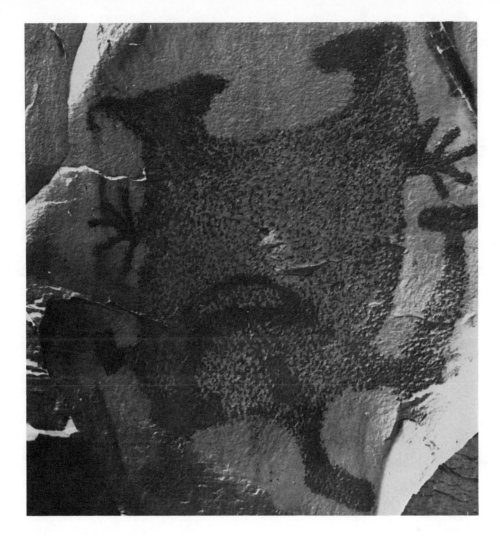

Area A

A Double composite style figure having facial features (eyes and mouth) inverted on the lower portion of its body. The figure has two sets of legs with feet and one pair of hands. There is an extra foot and part of a leg extending from the figure's lower right side. The general appearance of this figure is that of a person standing on their head, until you start to count the appendages.

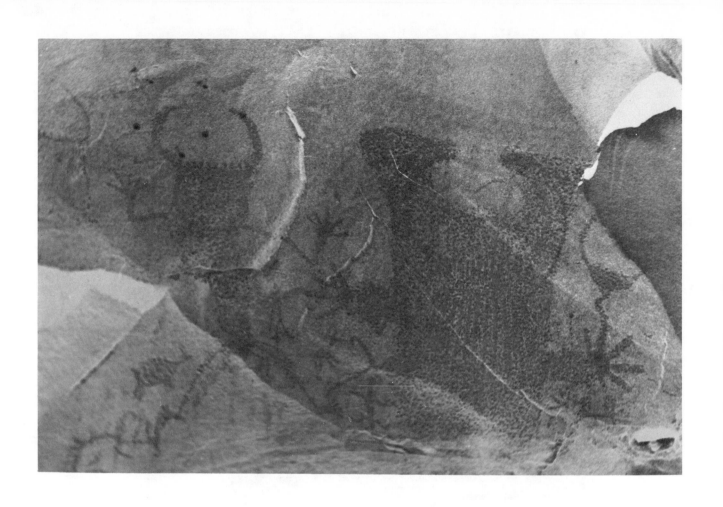

Area A

The figure on the right of the panel may be a repeat of the double composite described in the preceding photo.

Area A

There is much to see in this composite figure which is host to a smaller stick figure standing within the larger body. The feet and legs of the stick figure extend downward from the larger figure's body which is sectioned vertically. The heads of the host figure and the small one both have the "horned" or "crescent" style motif. In the lower portion of the host figure's body is a tiny spiral design. Meandering lines and the "wands" bearing crescent symbols are attached to a hand and an upper arm of the host figure. There are small animals and other human-like figures near the larger one.

Area A

The largest human figure on the panel is a double composite with a head in upright position and one inverted between spread legs. Other small human-like figures appear on the panel. Animals also appear near the large figure.

Area A

Host Satellite designs. The legs and feet of the human-like figures are in the characteristic spread leg posture. The patina on the cliff and boulders at this site is a deep brown which provided a sharp contrast for the art pecked there.

Area A

Area A

66

Human-like figural designs with smaller ones clustered or attached to a larger host figure were classified as Host-Satellite composites in the study.

Area A

A figure created at ground level. The "wand" with the crescent on the end extends from the lower body.

Area A

Large panel dominated by long bodied animals. Three have antlers. One has horns curled like a mountain sheep. The animal at lower left may be a doe. There is a human hand pecked at upper left and a human figure at lower right. The panel appears to have been created by one artist. The compositional style is similar to biographical hide painting.

Area A

Horned headdress/figure with its hand holding a horse.

Area A

Three double composite figures. The outline of a buffalo is at the left of the panel. A solidly pecked horse is "tied" to the foot of the figure at the far right.

Area A

The broken rock facing with dark brown patina has small animals across the top of the ledge and human-like figures with the horned or crescent head-style. The animal with long ears at upper left is a rabbit in the style of those painted on mortuary pottery of A.D. 900-1000, of the southwestern Mimbres culture. This is the only rabbit in the state inventory.

Area A

Larger than life size figure with sectioned body also having grid patterns at upper left and lower right on its body. At lower center, along one of the vertical lines, is a small horned, spread leg figure. Two buffalo are at lower right. There are bullet holes near the head, but no facial features indicated.

Area A

Detail of the buffalo of preceding photo.

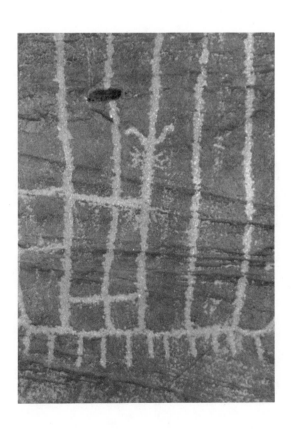

Area A

Detail of small horned figure on larger figure's lower body. (Preceding photo.)

Area A

Double composite design about five feet tall. The sectioned body has a curled design with hands in the center. The pelvic area between the feet has what appear to be two inverted heads, one above the other. Small human-like figures appear at lower right with a horse which has a crescent form over its head.

Area A

Detail of the inverted heads and lower portion of the figure in the preceding photo.

Area A

Area A

Double composite. The figure appears to have antlers until it is inverted.

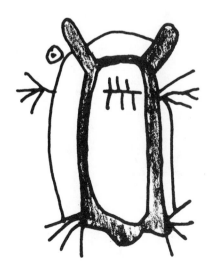
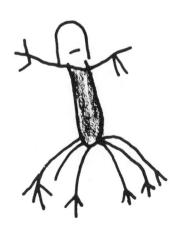

Area A

Two double composites. The one at the left has multiple arms and legs. The figure on the right of the panel is attached to an animal which is probably a horse.

Area A

The human-like figure with horned or crescent head-style is in the characteristic raised arm, spread-leg posture. The two depictions at the left of the panel may be birds.

Area A

Shadow type composite with two pair of arms. One arm on the left of the panel has partially weathered away. A long-bodied stick figure in raised arm posture appears at the upper breast area.

Area A

Tiny stylized figures at ground level nearly hidden by sagebrush. The figure on the left is a conventionalized double composite. The designs are about four inches tall.

Area A

Ground level figures near the panel in the preceding photo.

Area A

Shadow type composite. The zig-zag lines from the head to the oval-shaped enclosure of the figure are similar to the placement of zig-zag lines with two depictions at Castle Gardens in Area B. One of the Castle Garden depictions, a human figure enclosed in a circle, still remains; the other has been called the "great turtle" and was quarried from its panel. However, the turtle was recorded by Renaud in 1936.

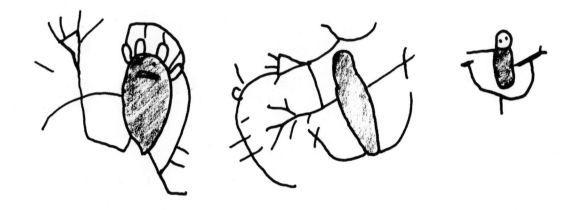

Area A

Closer view of human-like figure at upper right of the panel shown in the photo below. The morning star design appears between the feet of the figure.

Area A

Panel of pecked art on the end of a cliff at the entrance of a small canyon. Human figures are shown attached to horses.

Area A

Closer view of the conventionalized double figure at lower right of the panel shown in the preceding photo.

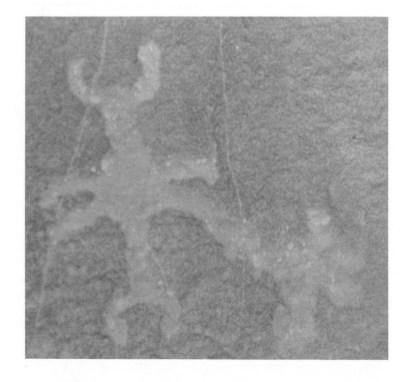

Area A

Shadow style composite. A very dense pecking forms an interior figure. Lighter pecking forms another figure around it. The large eyes appear above the head of the two interior figures creating another figure with the pecked outline. The lightly pecked figure has a small right arm with two fingers. Another arm with two fingers extends beyond the wider outside pecked line. On the left, an arm ending in a large hand with five long fingers and a short thumb extend from the lightly pecked interior figure.

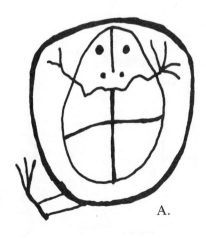

A.

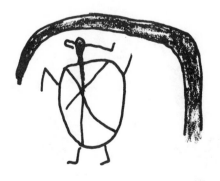

B.

Painted art; dark red; exposed cliff.

The design on the left is a shadow composite and also a double figure with an inverted head. Three horses are pecked below. The figure on the right side of the panel is a combination of double and host composite. Small figures appear on its body and at either side. Both figures are in the typical spread leg, raised arm posture.

The nearly life-sized pecked figure on the right of the panel is presented in the typical raised arm, spread leg posture, but is in a more recent and realistic style. The design which seems to be a sunburst, at the upper left of the panel, has a left hand with five fingers. The solidly pecked circle at center has arms and legs and two dots where the head might be expected.

Area A

Area A

Two figures by different art-makers illustrating two different interpretations of the spread-leg posture.

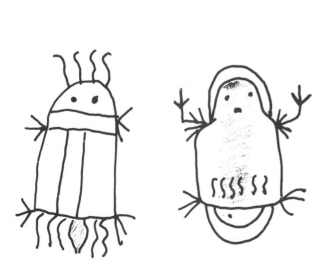

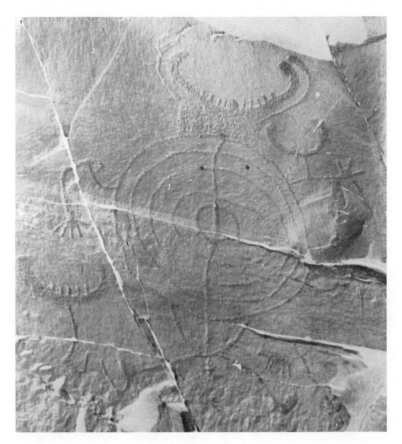

Area A

Area A

Pecked figure in the typical posture. The figure carries a bow in its right hand. A small conventionalized figure is below its left arm.

Area A

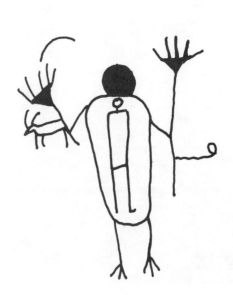

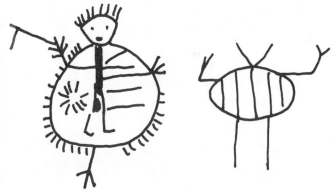

Area A

Area A

A large slab of fallen rock with both animals and human-like figures. The animals are probably horses. The animal at the left of the panel has a striped or sectioned body. The panel was created by different art-makers.

Area A

Closer view of two figures on the panel of preceding photo. The one on the left carries a bow. The one on the right is attached to a horse at foot and hand, and carries a "wand" with a crescent on one end and a double crescent on the lower end.

Area A

Shadow type composite design with six heads formed by a series of crescents above the solidly pecked interior body. The legs are in the spread position.

Area A

Area A

Composite style figure with a spear.

Area A

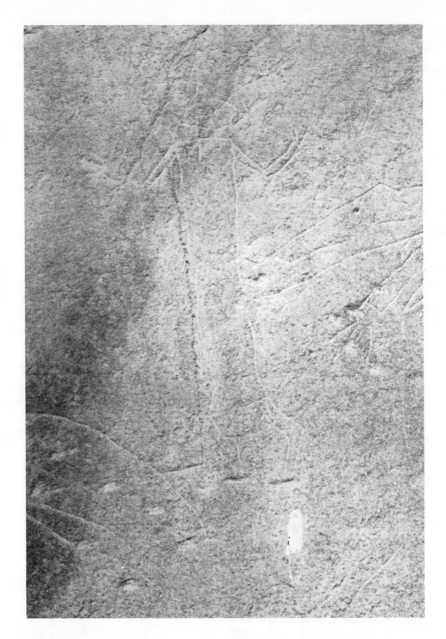

Area A

Long-bodied rectangular figure, incised. This style of figure is typical of the art in the eastern part of the state and of the historic Great Plains period. There are two animals on either side of the figure. (See next two photos.)

Area A

Animal at the right side of the figure in the preceding photo. Probably a buffalo.

Area A

Animal at the left of the figure described above. The long head of the animal may indicate that it is a horse.

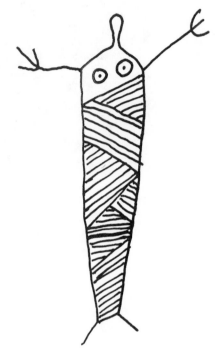

Drawing shows figure in Photo A.

Area A

An incised figure with a small head which has weathered on one side. The body appears to be wrapped by cloth although articles of clothing are not characteristic on rock art figures in Wyoming.

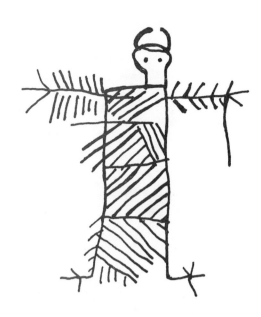

Area A

Incised human-like figure appearing on the same panel as the figure of the preceding photo. The art-maker probably attempted to copy the figure in its wrapped style body.

Area A

Abraded, pecked and incised abstract designs with one pecked mountain sheep. The design across the bottom of the photo may be what Mallery and others have identified as appearing in Winter Count hide paintings.

Area A

Double composite, solidly pecked. Someone has chalked the design and their interpretation ignores and obscures details. However, the inverted head is well-defined. The animal at the figure's left is probably a horse.

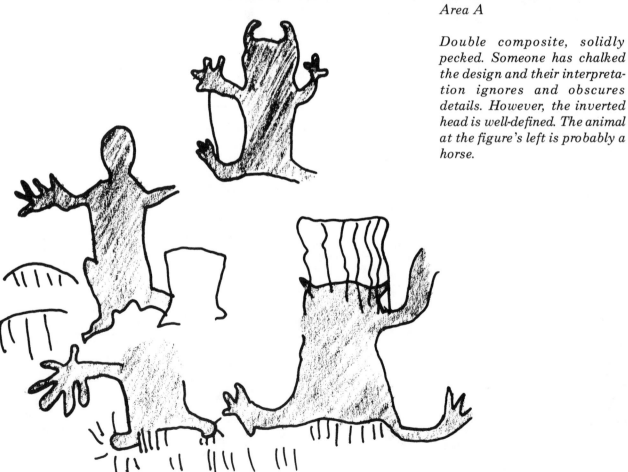

Area A

Human-like figure in the typical spread leg posture. An animal, probably a horse, is pecked at the left of the panel near the figure's head.

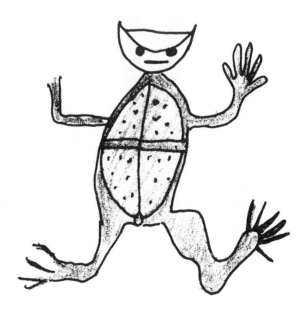

Area A

The surface of this sandstone cliff has flaked away leaving traces of the art once created there. At lower left is an animal which has the characteristics of a mountain lion. Mountain lions appear in the art in the southern part of Area A and in the northern part of Area B.

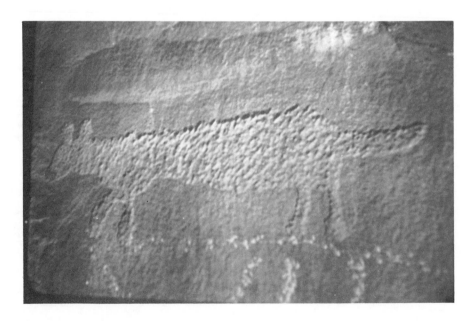

Area A

Mountain lion. The feet are paw-shaped.

Area A

Human-like figure with sectioned body. Several small animals (mountain sheep) appear on the panel along with one pecked human handprint and the mysterious design at the left.

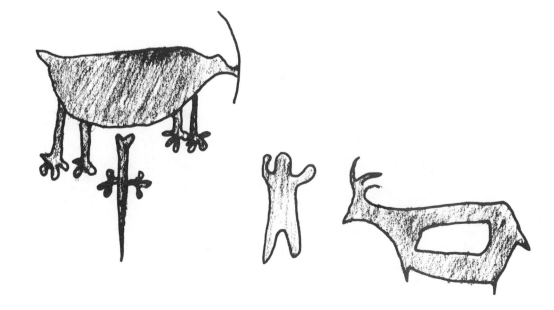

Area A

Human-like figure with wings and horned headstyle. A smaller figure is pecked at upper right.

Area A

This composite is nearly life-size. It has a small figure sticking out of its right side. The other projection is probably another figure although it is not as well defined. The three slash marks below the pelvis are repeated on a nearby boulder.

Area A

Partially abraded technique combined with pecking. The composite has two pair of legs, but only two arms with hands. The figure's left leg is incomplete.

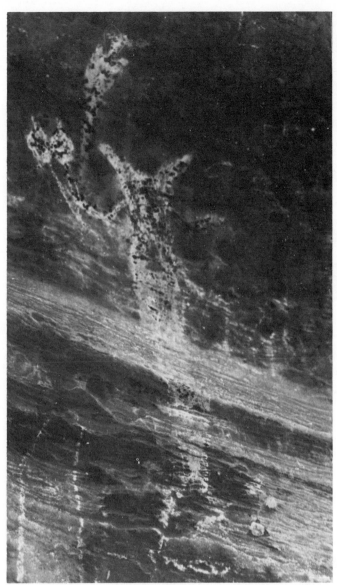

Area A

A red painted figure with a "keyhole" design left unpainted on its breast. It holds a pair of rattles in one hand. The figure is painted in a deep cave near the ceiling.

Painted art; red; deep cave.

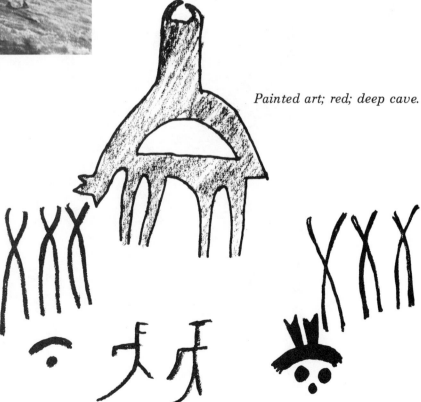

101

Area A

Bear created with charcoal. The feet, snout and side of the animal are daubed with white pigment. The pattern of the daubs of paint appear to have been made with a piece of fur. Cave painting.

Area A

Charcoal painting of a buffalo with a series of slash marks below it. Cave painting.

A Ghost Dance style bird with a human-like figure attached to the bird's left foot. The figure is in the typical posture and has a sectioned body. The panel appears on a large isolated boulder at the edge of a narrow creek.

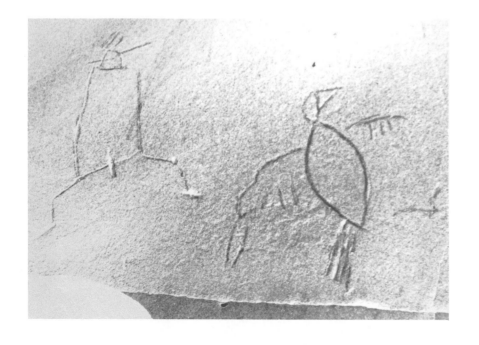

Area A

Human-like figure in typical posture with a Ghost Dance style bird. Both designs are incised although pecked technique is characteristic of Area A rock art.

Area A

Ghost Dance style bird at the left. Human-like figures and an animal which has two tails also appear on the panel.

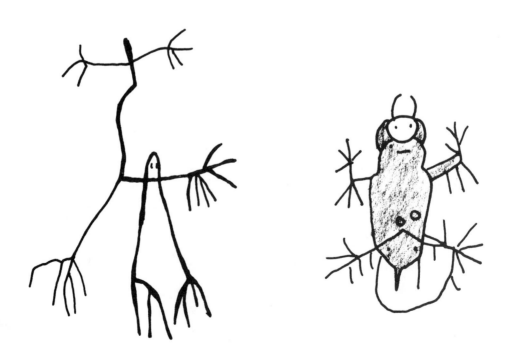

Area A

Three birds. The two top ones do not have the typical spread wings. The lower one is in the style of Ghost Dance birds.

Area A

Two Ghost Dance style birds with spread wings. The bird on the left appears to have been made more recently.

Area A

Ghost Dance style bird at the top with a horned human-like figure below. The arms of the lower figure may represent wings or other satellite figures.

Area A, Northeast.

Area A, Northeast.

Area A, Northeast

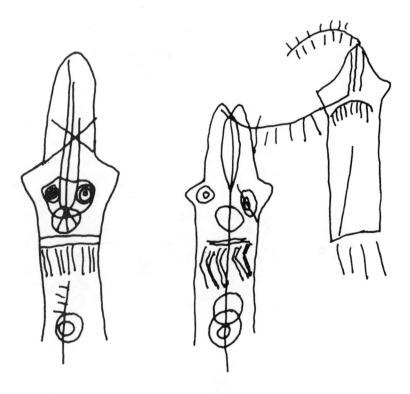

Area A, Northeast

Circular and rectangular bodied composite. The arms are raised in the typical pose, but the legs and feet are turned toward the figure's right. The horizontal line which represents the arms is repeated across the lower section of the body ending in what may be another pair of hands or feet.

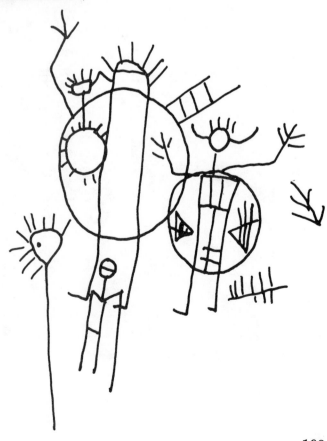

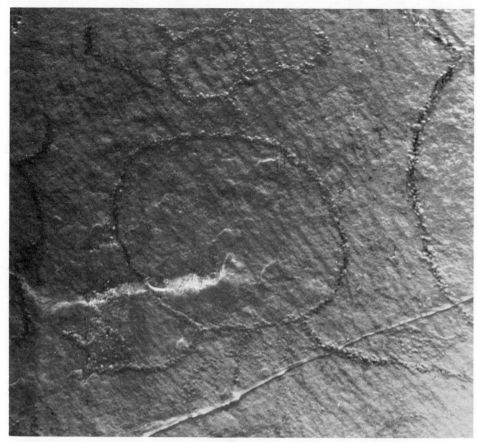

Area A, Northeast.
Circular bodied figure in the spread leg posture characteristic of the southern part of Area A and Area B.

Area A, Northeast.

These figures are in the style of those appearing in Winter Counts painted on tanned buffalo hides by the Sioux during the 1800's.

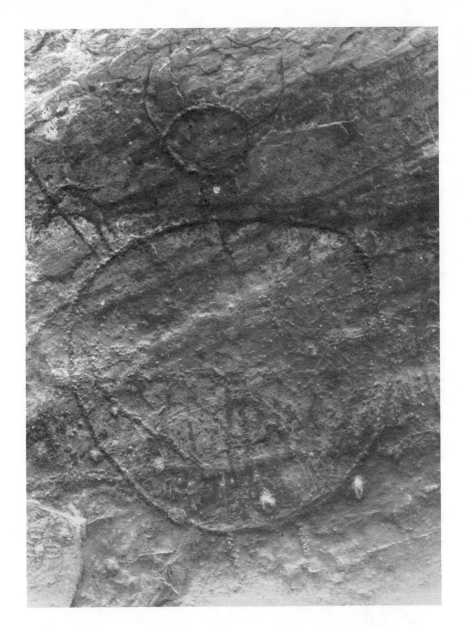

Area A, Northeast.

Round bodied host style composite with small figures on lower body. Legs and feet are turned toward the figure's right.

Painted art; black with circular daubs of white; deep cave.

Area A, Northeast.

The depiction in this red painted art has been called a deer with tracks forming a circle around it. If it is a deer, it is the only one in the rock art inventory with the head and antlers turned forward on a profile body.

Area A, Northeast.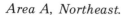

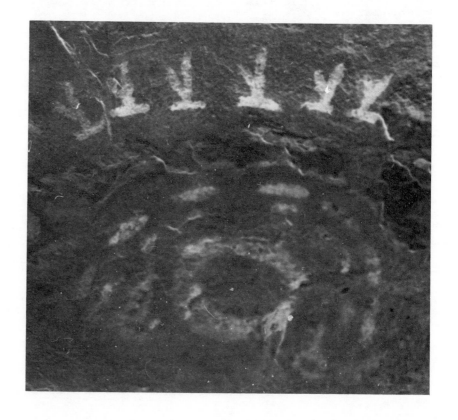

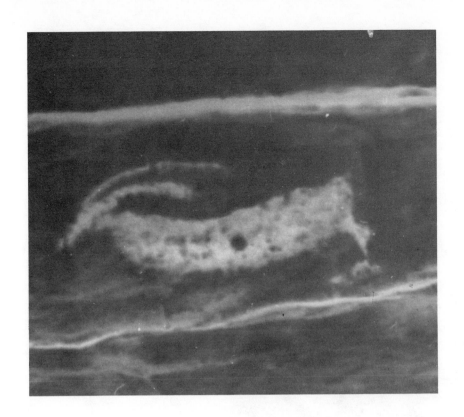

Area A, Northeast.

A long-bodied animal with back-curving horns. The depiction was created with charcoal and has a white disk on its side. (The printing of the photo was reversed to bring out details.)

Area A, Northeast.

Part of a line of animals having horns like mountain sheep. The animals are solidly painted at head and shoulders and divided by a vertical line at mid-section.

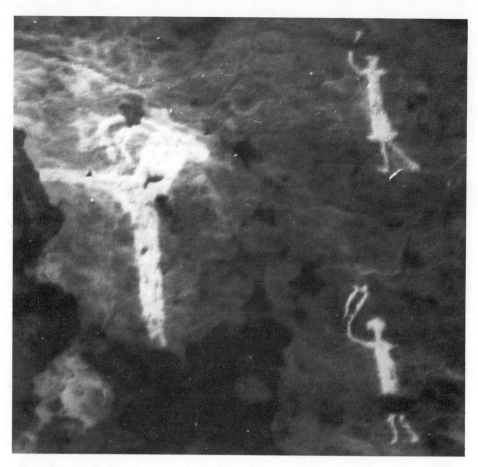

Area A, Northeast.

Two human figures painted with a dark red-brown pigment under a protective ledge. The figures are unique in Wyoming rock art. Both figures are holding something above their heads, and both are missing their left arms. (The photo was printed in reverse to illustrate details.)

Painted art; red; deep rock shelter.

114

Area A, Northeast.

Circular style body with crescents arranged in several positions on its body. The body is divided by a vertical line from the breast to the lower crescent. The head has what appear to be large round ears giving it a Mickey Mouse appearance. However, the "ears" are probably a hair style.

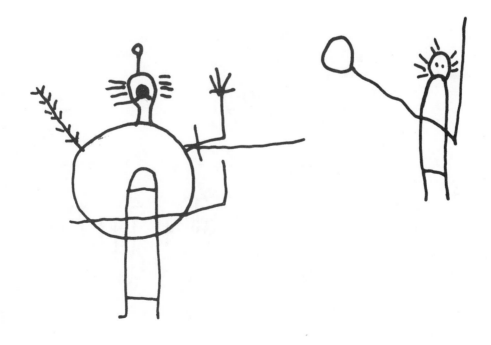

Area A, Northeast.

The elk or deer in the photo is the largest antlered animal ever recorded in the state inventory. The animal is seven feet and seven inches long from nose to tail. The animal has several large arrows penetrating its body.

Area A, Northeast.

Detail of the head of the elk or deer in the preceding photo. There are four other large animals identified as buffalo at this site. The four are not detailed and consist of a pecked outline. The largest of the buffalo is about six feet long.

Area A, Northeast.

Pecked line animal with a gullet.

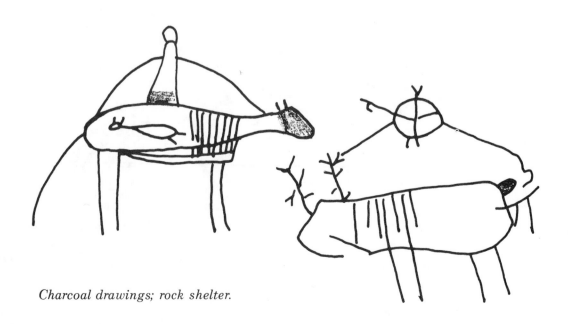

Charcoal drawings; rock shelter.

Area A, Northeast.

Incised depiction of a campsite with lodges arranged around a large circle. This is the only "landscape" in the state inventory. The two animals within the circle of lodges are probably horses.

White painted man on horseback. The design in front of the horse may be a bear track.

119

Area A, Northwest.

The body of this figure is unique in Wyoming rock art. It is turned in three-quarter profile with the head in frontal position. The depiction is about six feet tall and has two arrows through its body. The figure has a nose and eyebrows which are not characteristic in Wyoming rock art. Larger bear tracks, small human figures and animals appear nearby.

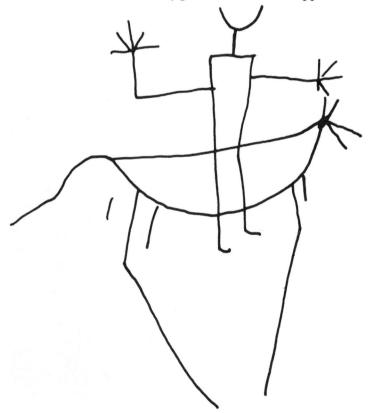

Area A

Double composite. The lower head is solidly pecked. The eyes are difficult to determine on the inverted head, but the mouth is easily discerned. The figure is host to a stick figure with the spread-leg posture, at center of its body.

Area A

Satellite composite style design.

Area A

Pecked human-like figure. Between the two pecked figures with horned or crescent head-style, is a lightly incised human-like figure with a V-necked, rectangular style body typical of Areas C, D, E and F (Map #1) in Wyoming. The style is also characteristic of the Great Plains historic period.

Area A

Area A

An isolated boulder with two human-like figures on their sides. One figure at the right, is surrounded by a series of concentric circles. The figure at the left is attached to the outside circle of the other figure. Above both figures, at the top edge of the boulder, is a life size depiction of a human hand with part of the arm. The arm and hand are not attached to any figure.

Area A

Two pecked line composites with a small horse solidly pecked below. This relationship of very small animals with large human-like figures is typical in Areas A and B, when animals are depicted.

Area B

Area B

The often-photographed panel at Dinwoody in the Wind River Mountains on the west side of the Wind River Indian Reservation.

Area B

Detail of the lower left part of the panel in the preceding photo.

Area B

Detail of figures at the right side of the panel described above.

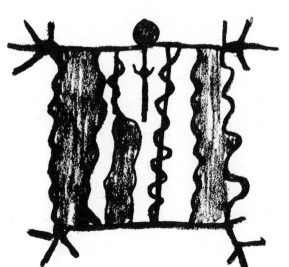

This illustration is a composite human-like figure from the main Dinwoody panel, lower right.

Area B

Dinwoody site. The large design is a human-like figure on its side.

Area B
Dinwoody.

Area B

Dinwoody site. Both figures at the right have small ones in upright position at the pelvis between the legs.

Area B

Area B

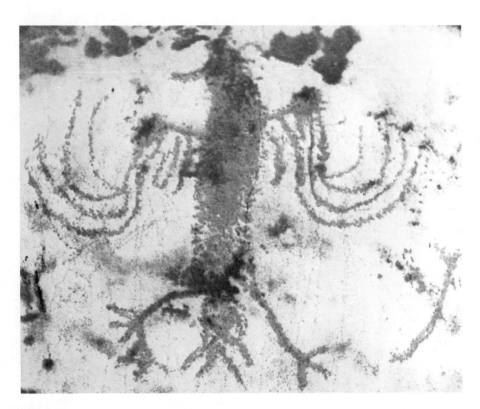

Area B

Area B

Area B

Area B

133

Area B

Shadow type composite with a small figure at the pelvis between spread legs of the large figure.

Area B

Shadow composite style design.

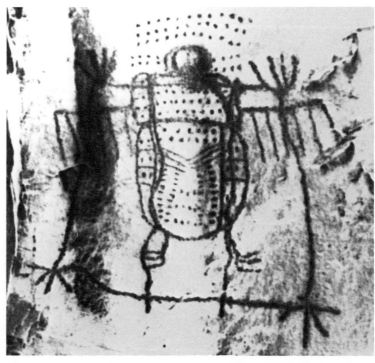

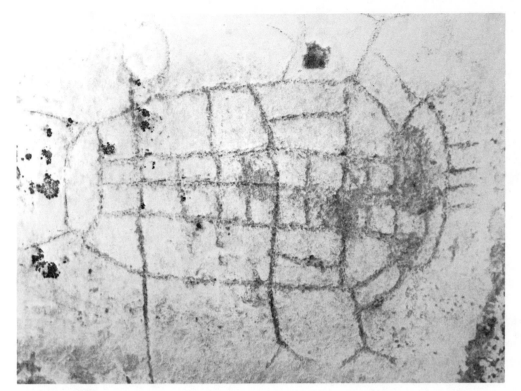

Area B

Shadow composite with a solidly pecked interior figure. The composite has multiple arms and legs indicating other figures merged with the larger one.

Area B

Double composite with multiple arms or legs.

135

Area B

Shadow type composite style design with a head indicated on the breast. The figure may also be a double composite with an inverted head having a fan-shaped headdress below the pelvis. The triple lines from the lower legs are probably an interpretation of the model figure of Photo 17, described in the text.

Area B

The large figure is host to a small one on its breast.

Area B

Shadow composite with small figures on its interior.

Area B

An isolated, eroded section of sandstone cliff photographed from an adjoining hill. Two power line poles are shown in the distance beyond the cliff. The cliff has rock art depictions on all sides.

Area B

The main panel appearing on the cliff described in the photo above. The shadow style composite design at the left is discussed under composite style design in the text. (Also see Fig. 26.)

138

Area B

Closer view of the figure on the right side of the panel in Photo B., preceding photo. Note footprints on the body of the figure.

Area B

Several styles of composite designs appear on this panel. The two lower center figures are double composites with inverted heads at the pelvis.

140

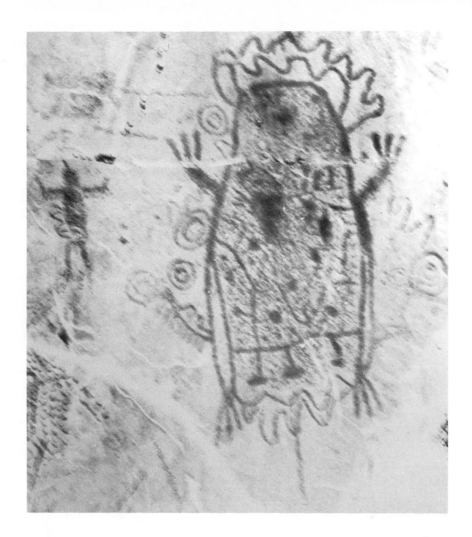

Area B

Host composite.

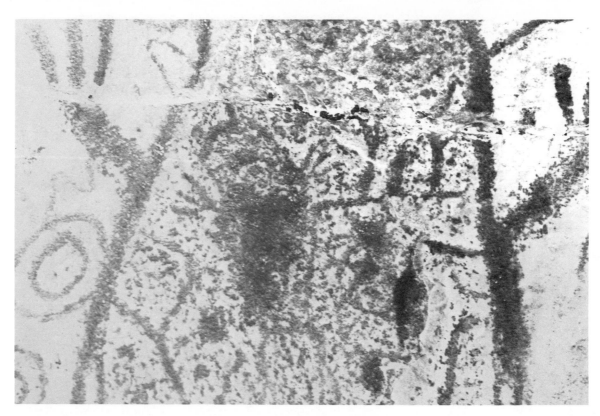

Area B

Detail of the small solidly pecked figure on the breast of the figure in preceding photo.

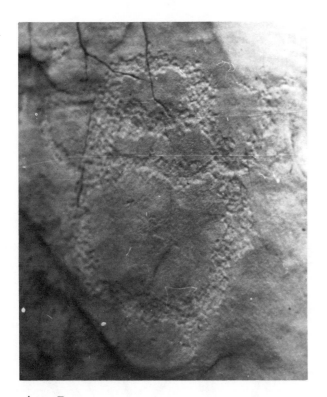
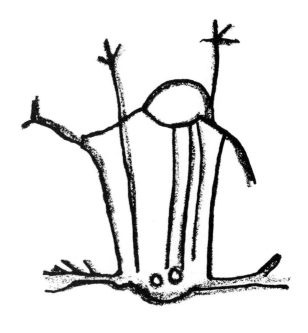

Area B

Double composite.

Area B

Among the abstract symbols on the body of this figure is the morning star on the breast.

Area B

This petroglyph has been called a bird, but it is probably a human with an inverted crescent at mid-breast and over its head.

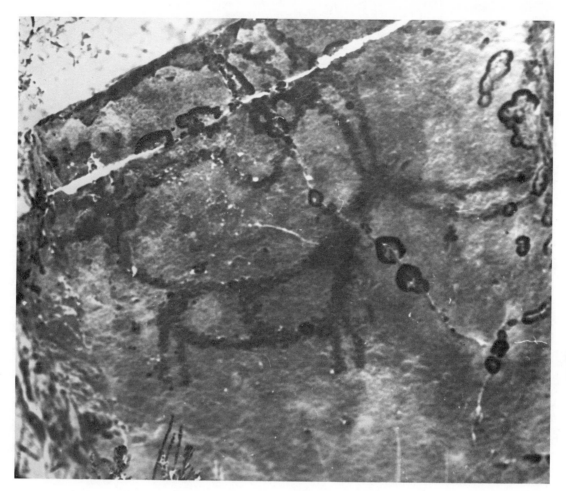

Area B

This animal with a long head and mouth is probably a horse.

Area B

Area B

Two composites on a boulder near a lake. The figure at upper right is a host composite.

Area B

Detail from the preceding photo showing the small figures on the upper breast of the large figure described.

146

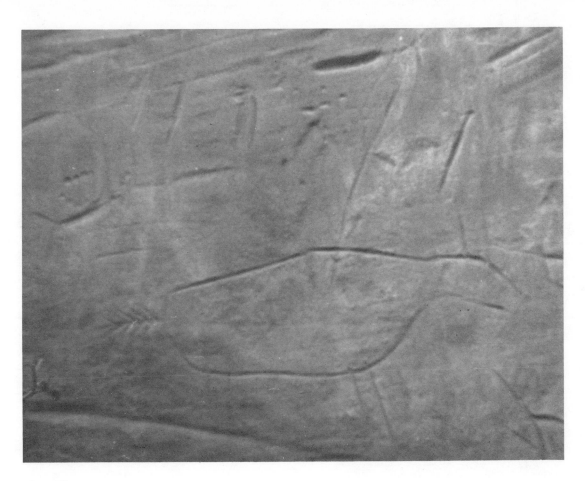

Area B

Incised horse with a feather or arrow in its back.

Area B

Pecked composite design of a human with a horse at mid-section of its body.

Area B

Double composite.

Area B

Rocks broken from the cliffs above. A pecked figure, at center, is on the smooth facing of one rock which is somewhat sheltered between the others.

Area B

The large figure with a small one attached to its right arm, pecked on the rock described in the photo above.

Area B

Area B

Detail of figure at center of preceding photo. The figure is a shadow style composite with a solidly pecked figure at the center and two circular shadow figures around it.

Area B

Double composite on the left of the panel.

Area B

Shadow composites at ground level.

Area B

Two human-like figures by the same art-maker. The left one is in upright position and the right one is inverted. Other figures are pecked on the bodies of both.

Area B

Two figures in the spread-leg posture. A horse is pecked at the right of the panel near the figure.

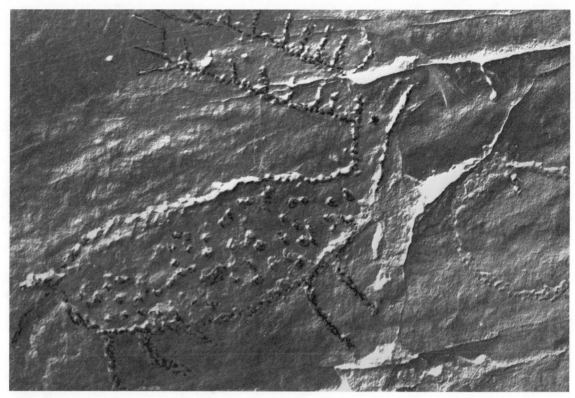

Area B

Elk or deer. The art has been chalked by an unknown photographer.

Area B

A large elk or deer with small figures. The three figures on the panel have inverted crescents over their heads.

Area B

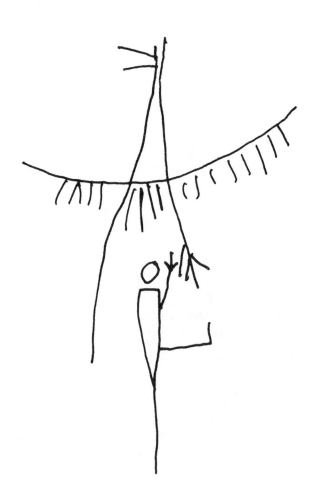

154

Area B

Incised and pecked techniques appearing on the same panel. The pecked figures at the center are typical of Area A.

Area B

Detail of a pecked figure among the incised art at the site described above.

Area B

Two nearly life-sized figures. Both were probably made by the same artist. The one on the left is not pecked as deeply as the one on the right. The legs are in the typical posture, but the arms hang downward.

Area B

Closer view of the figure on the right side of the panel described in the preceding photo.

156

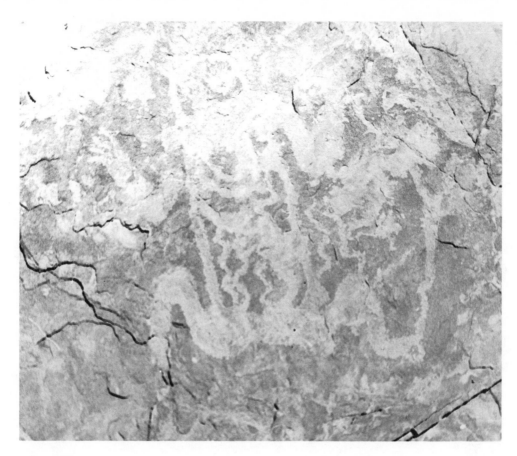

Area B

Figure on a badly weathered isolated boulder. The figure has a crescent design extending from its left foot.

Area B

An incised shadow type composite.

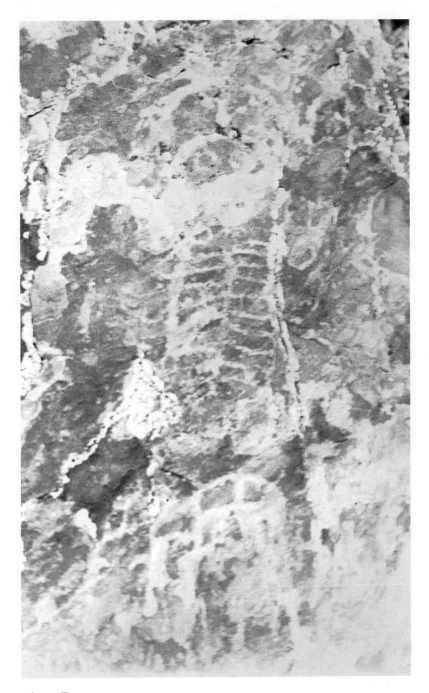

Area B

Isolated boulder with a large pecked figure which has a smaller one in upright position below its pelvis.

Area B

Area B

Shadow style composite.

160

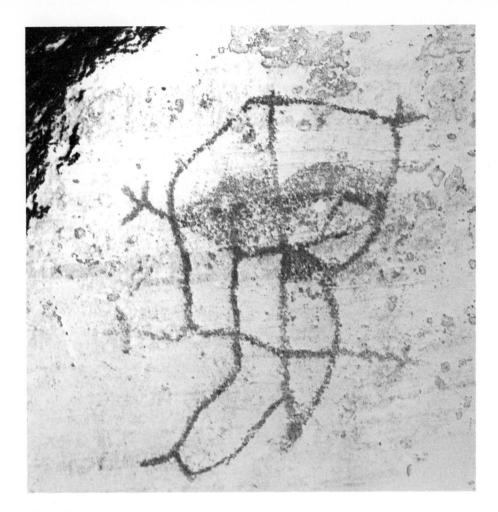

Area B

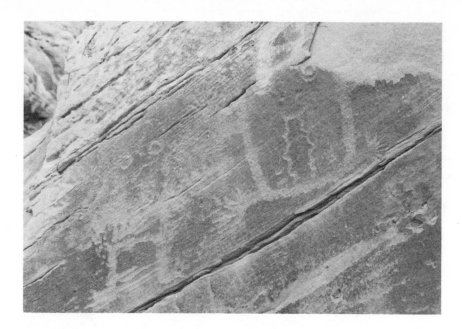

Area B

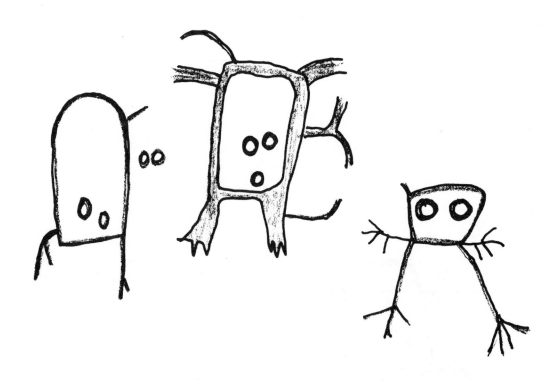

Area B

An isolated boulder with a human-like design.

Area B

Closer view of the design on the panel of the preceding photo.

Area B

Two life size figures in the characteristic pose. The faces of both figures are divided by horizontal bands of pecking. This motif is not common in Wyoming rock art. Vandals have fired several bullets into the panel.

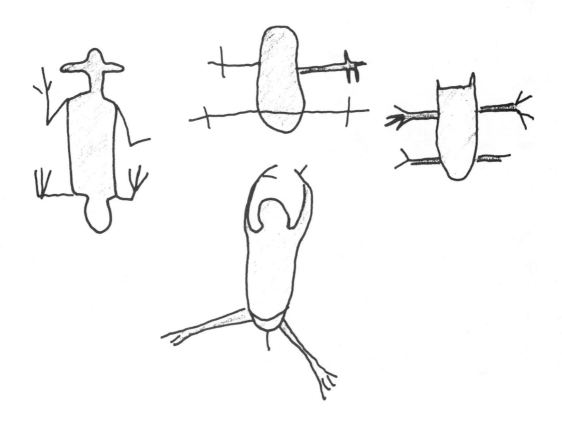

Area B

Area B

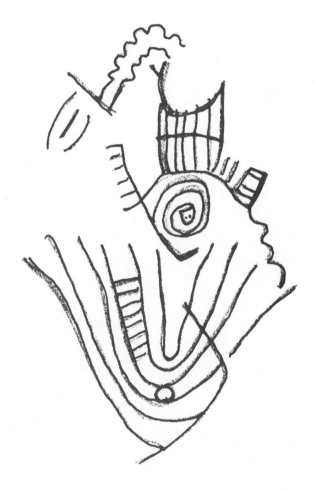

Area B

Area B

166

Drawings from photographs by Sowers, 1939. These petroglyphs were near Boysen Lake in central Wyoming.

Area B

Incised, vertical rectangular figures joined together in the genital area. The figure on the right in the photo carries a crescent.

Area B

Incised slashes and dots.

Area B

This animal has often been mistaken for a bird. However, it is a mountain sheep with the head and horns on the right side of the photo. It has an arrow or a feather sticking out of its back. The depiction is at Castle Garden.

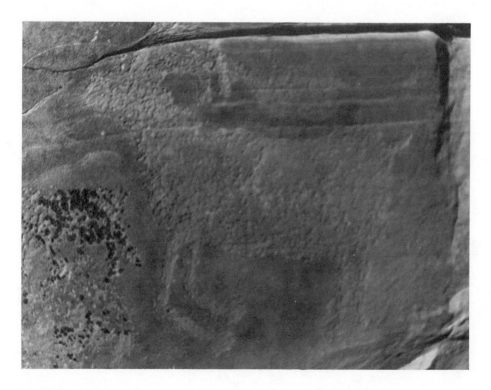

Area B

Solidly pecked mountain sheep with typical back-curving horns.

Area B

Elk or deer with an abraded body and incised line legs and antlers.

Area B

Human-like figure, incised. Illustration of the figure is shown below.

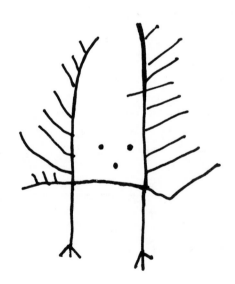

Area B

Area B

Ghost Dance style birds at Castle Garden.

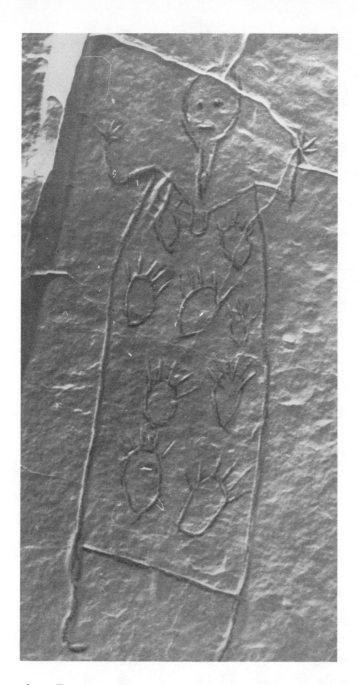

An illustration of a figure which also has human footprints on its body.

Area B

(Castle Garden) A v-necked, rectangular bodied composite with footprints which probably indicate additional humans merged with the larger one. Chalking by an unknown vandal has distorted the figure by ignoring the mark at the pelvis and the motif attached to the head.

Area B

(Castle Garden) Circular designs with interior depictions of animals, humans and abstract symbols. These have been referred to as shields by some rock art investigators. However, the shields of Plains Indians of the 1800's were decorated with sacred medicine fetishes which had appeared to the shield owners in visions or dreams. The symbols applied to the shields were believed to have great supernatural protective powers quite aside from perhaps deflecting arrows or bullets of the enemy. Care was taken to keep the shields covered with specially prepared and decorated animal skin to keep the shield's medicine powers from being seen by the enemy and casual observers. For that reason it seems doubtful that warriors would create their shield designs in a "public" place. These designs are probably late-style interpretations of circular design composite symbolism.

Area B

(Castle Garden) Closer view of one of the circular composite designs. The vertical line through the center of the large circle has two legs, a small head and two arms.

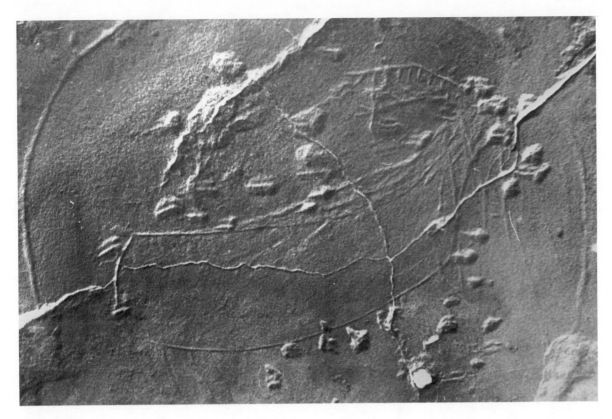

Area B

(Castle Garden) Circular design containing an antlered animal, probably an elk because of the markings on the head and shoulders of the animal.

Area B

(Castle Garden) Circular composite containing a human-like head with horns and nine vertical marks which may represent hair or have some symbolic meaning. Small human-like figures in the raised arm, spread leg posture also appear in the circle.

Area B

(Castle Garden) Bird design near the circular designs previously shown.

Area B

Very large animal with nine vertical lines divided by a horizontal line. The motif may indicate the animal's ribs. The spiral in the belly area may represent a symbol or it may indicate intestines. The spiral appears infrequently in Wyoming rock art, but usually with human-like figures.

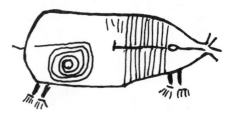

Illustration of the animal in the preceding photograph.

176

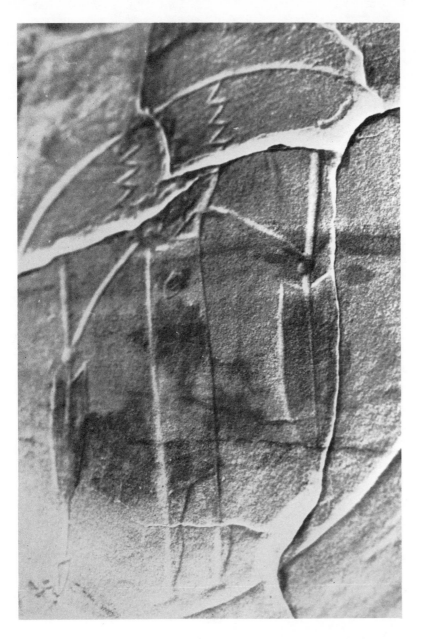

Area B

(Castle Garden)

This figure was recorded by Renaud fifty years ago. He called it a warrior and described painted areas in the design. The photograph was made in 1978. The illustration accompanying this photo was re-drawn from Renaud and shows areas shaded to indicate green, yellow and red painting. As of this date (fifty years later) there are only faint traces of color remaining. The colors can be detected by spraying the design with a fine mist of clean water. Note the incised circle or disk on the figure's breast.

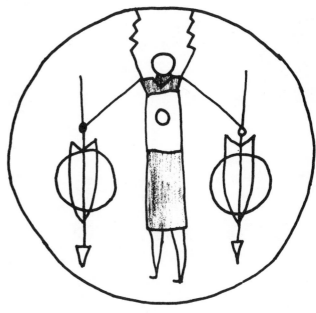

Area C

Area C

Incised panel of art by several different art-makers.

Area C

This figure appears at center of the photo above. The stick figure is a composite design with two right arms and three left arms. The legs are in the typical spread posture.

181

Area C

An elk or deer and a bear. Bears are usually presented in profile, in upright position with all four legs forward.

Area C

Humans with guns.

182

Area C

Detail from large panel. Note the human-like composite figure on horseback at the left.

Area C

Human footprint. One of several at the same site. There are also bear tracks at the site.

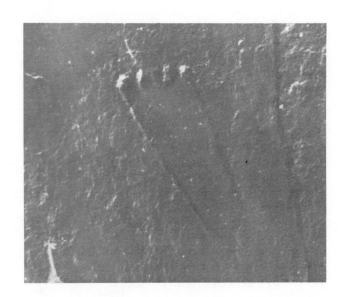

Area C

Elk and mountain sheep.

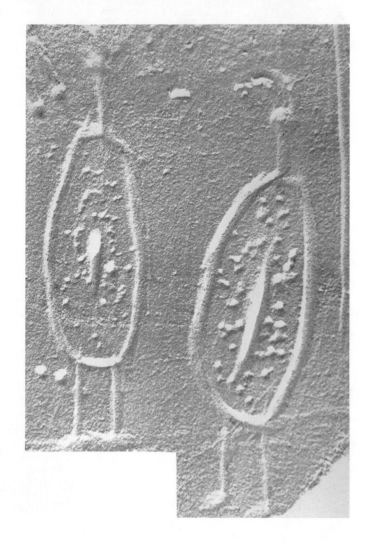

Area C

Incised human-like figures having one feather, one horn or one braid of hair. Note random pecking on the bodies.

Area C

Area C

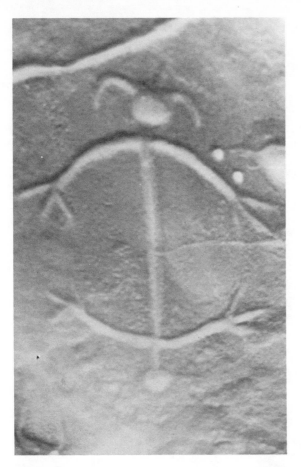

Area C

Double composite, incised.

Area C

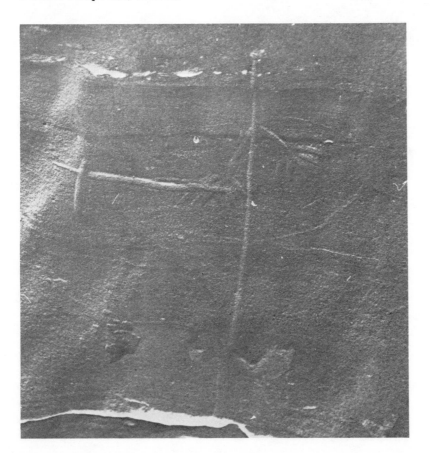

186

Area C

Incised animals, probably horses.

Area C

Incised elk or deer with both eyes on one side of the head.

Area C
At upper right are two incised rectangular figures in the spread-leg posture typical of Areas A and B pecked figures.

Area C

Incised figures, some with braids, and the cedar or pine bough motif.

Area C
Buffalo.

Area C
Buffalo.

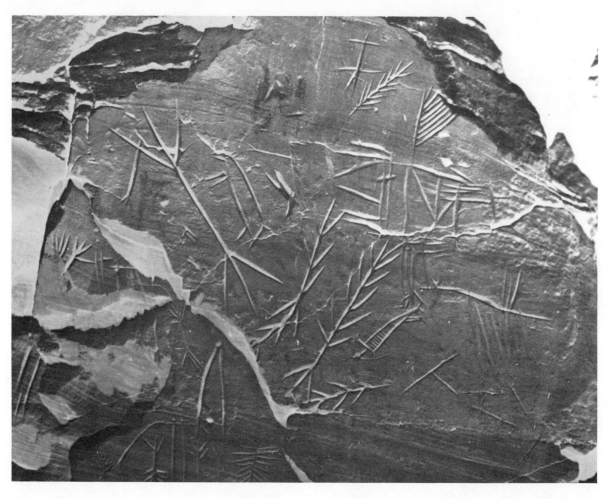

Area C

Total panel of incised art probably created by one artist. Sites in the same general area also have examples of the "cedar bough" motif. There is a bear just left of center.

Area C:

Detail of the panel in the photo above showing the inverted (fallen or dead) figure which has one arm and a sectioned breast. A long braid or feather hangs from the head.

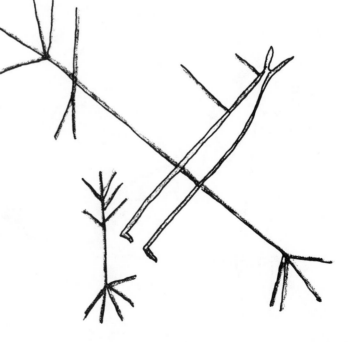

Area C:

Horned headdress figure on horseback. At the upper right of the panel is a different style human figure with the "weeping eye" motif common in Utah rock art. The motif is rare in Wyoming with only two examples recorded.

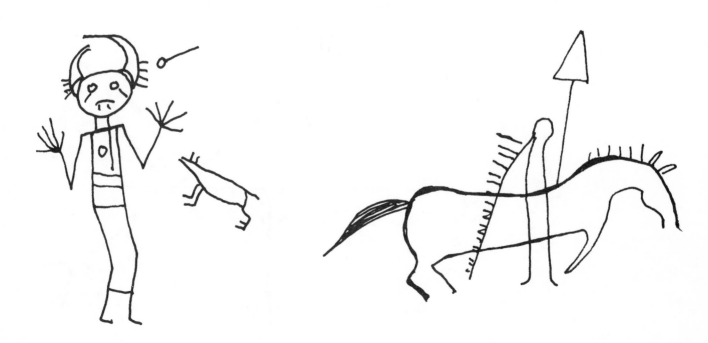

Area C

Two interpretations of the morning star symbol incised on the low ceiling of a small rock shelter.

Area C

Biographical hide painting style composition by one art-maker using one tool throughout. At center is a conventionalized bird. An animal, probably a horse, is at the left. Several human figures appear below.

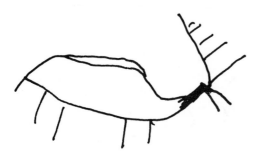

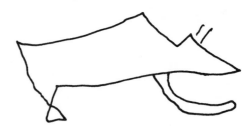

194

Area C

This site is south of Area C, just over the Colorado state line. It is in a twisted canyon with steep walls above a seasonally dry creek bed. The subjects are game animals including buffalo, mountain sheep and deer. Two horses appear among the other animals. Some of the subjects depicted on the panel are humans. Some of these figures carry bows. The compositional style is similar to that of biographical painting on hides.

Area C

Drawing of two composite designs in the figural style of Areas C, D, E, and F. The figure on the left is a Host composite with a small figure at its pelvis in upright position. An arrow crosses the small figure's breast. Note that the legs of the large figure are in the style characteristic of Areas A and B. A variation of the morning star design appears below the figure's left hand and a circle encloses the right one. The figure on the right of the drawing, is a Double composite with a different variation of the morning star near its leg. The diamond-shape has also been interpreted as meaning "navel" when it appears without the + design within it.

Area D

Area D

Bird deeply incised on a fallen boulder.

Area D
Pecked figure.

Area D

Deeply grooved circular bodied style human figures.

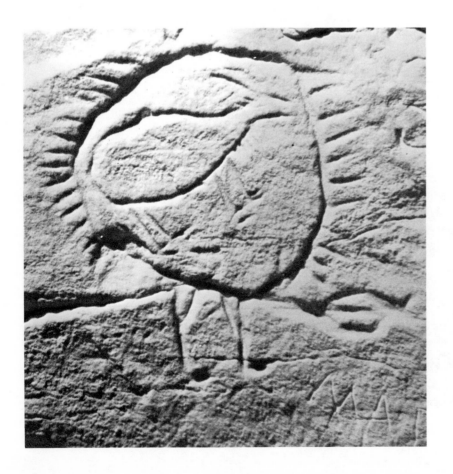

Area D

Circular bodied composite with an animal.

Area D

Vertical rectangular style figures.

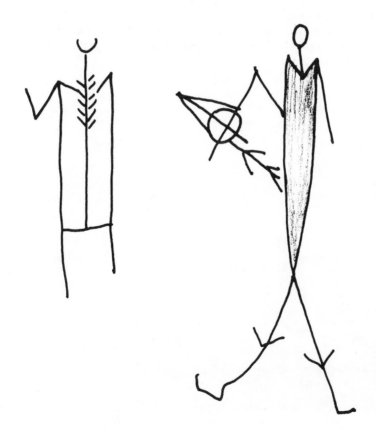

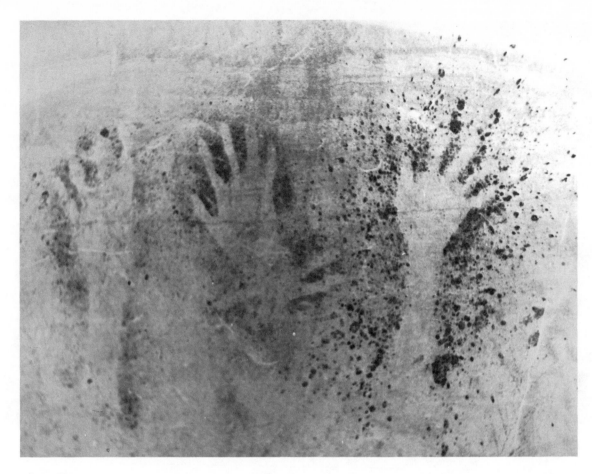

Area D

Human handprints stenciled in yellow clay. The clay was probably obtained from the nests of swallows fastened under the rim of the high rock shelter. There are hand prints of all sizes at the site and incised human figures in the rectangular bodied V-necked style. There are numerous handprints in the state inventory. Some are pecked, some incised, some painted; but these are the only clay stenciled ones. Handprints created by this technique are common in the American Southwest.

Area D

Composite style circular and rectangular style figure. An interpretation of the morning star symbol appears near the figure on the right of the panel.

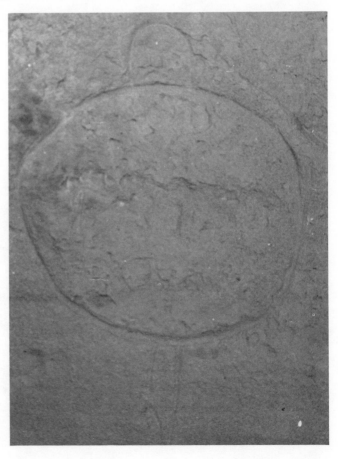

Area D

203

Area D

Incised animal, probably a horse. There appear to be several arrows in the abdomen of the animal. The diamond-shaped motifs above the back of the horse and near its front feet are variations of the morning star symbol used in the Ghost Dance of 1890-92. What appears to be a cedar bough motif is at the left side of the photo. The site has been vandalized by someone using a brown felt tip pen.

Area D

Another section of the cliff in the photo above. Slash marks and the cedar bough symbol predominate.

Area D

Human stick figure in the spread leg posture, but with arms downward. The figure has been traced with a brown felt tip pen marker.

Area D

Circular bodied figure with grid pattern. Slash marks are at figure's left. The animal appears to be charging the figure. Note the drilled holes above the two depictions.

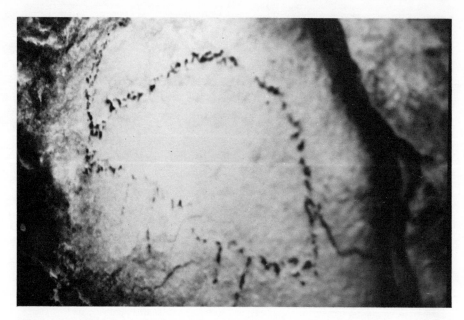

Area D

Charcoal drawing of a buffalo in a cave.

Area D

Charcoal drawing of an elk or deer in the same cave as the buffalo in the preceding photo.

Area D

A raised ledge under a long rock shelter. The shelter has numerous depictions along its walls and near the ceiling. There is some pecking at the site, but the characteristic technique is incised line. The site has been vandalized by someone using a brown felt tip pen probably in an attempt to photograph the art. Some of the depictions are distorted in the photographs because of the crude brown markings. Attempts to remove the brown ink from the stone failed.

Area D

Animals on the panel of the shelter described above.

Area D

Other art in the shelter described.

Area D

Incised and pecked composite.

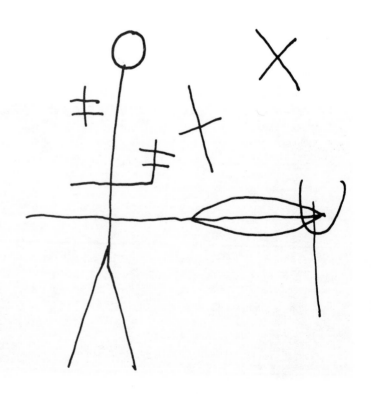

208

Area D

Rectangular bodied figure, incised technique. The figure in the center of the photo is host to a small figure below the waist, in upright position. A horse is left of the figure.

Area D

Incised rectangular figure with a small stick figure in upright position between its legs.

Area D

Double composite style stick figure in horizontal position. The human-like design is enclosed by a form which resembles a bear track with claws on the left.

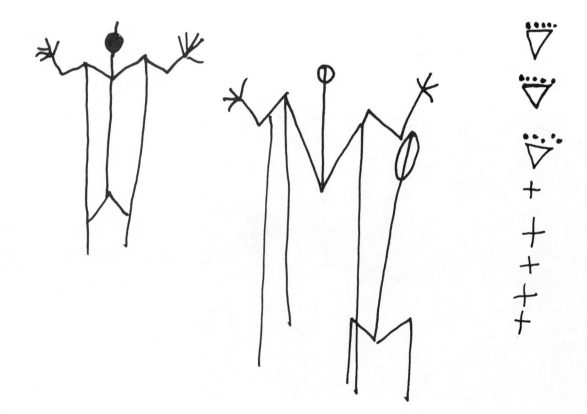

Area D

Panel of drawings and paintings on the ceiling of a rock shelter. The figure at lower left is a double composite in the characteristic posture. The figure in horizontal position is painted on the ceiling in charcoal and has a red disk painted on its breast. An inverted figure appears above the latter described one.

Area D

Two depictions from the panel described above. The two round drawings may be turtles.

Area D

Three women in the photograph give some idea of the size of the rock which has fallen from the cliff above. One corner on the left is broken forming a small crevice-like shelter. There is a panel of art on the facing near the entrance to the shelter and a panel with one figure within.

Area D

Human figure with an animal attached by a long line. This panel is near the entrance to the shelter described above.

Area D

Human-like figure pecked inside the crevice-shelter described above. The figure is in the spread-leg, raised arm posture and similar to the figures of Areas A and B. The drawing accompanying the photo shows detail of the figure.

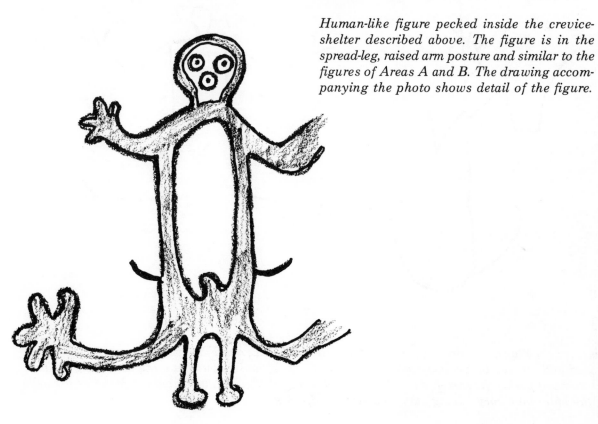

Area D

Figures across the top of the drawing are typical in Areas C, D, E, and F, Map #1. The two lower figures are incised and created in the body styles of Areas C, D, E, and F, but have the spread-leg posture characteristic of pecked figures in Area A and B, Map #1. All figures illustrated are found at the only site in the state inventory having clay stenciled handprints.

214

Area E

Area E

Long bodied, stick figures in the spread leg, raised arm posture. Morning star symbols and slash marks are scatterd among the figures. There is one double style composite figure near the center of the photo.

Area E

A small panel of stick figures in the spread leg, raised arm posture. The site is on a low rock ledge over a narrow little stream.

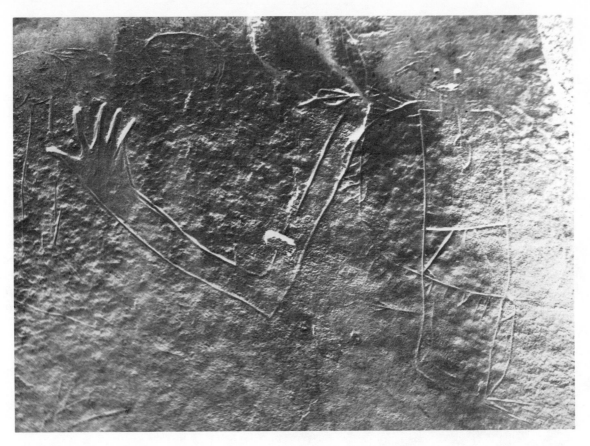

Area E

The large abraded and incised arm and hand are not attached to any figure. The rectangular bodied figure at the right of the photo has arms and hands and is enclosed by a large feathered circle. The figure's right leg is pierced by an arrow.

Area E

A circular bodied figure with vertical sectioning on its left side. There are numerous arrows penetrating the body. The head has a nose. Noses are not characteristic in Wyoming rock art.

Area E

Cliff facing with numerous small animals and human figures. There are three 1890-92 Ghost Dance style birds on this panel. The animals include elk or deer, buffalo and horses.

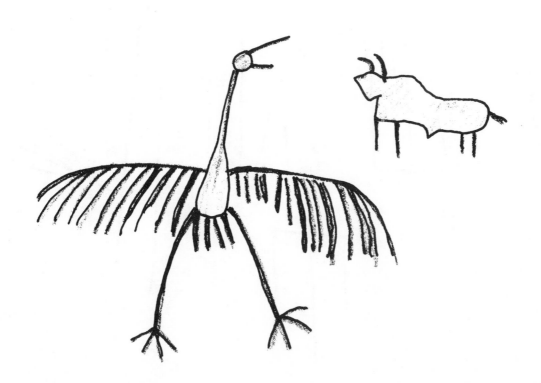

Area E

Antlered animals and humans. One figure is prepared to shoot an arrow from his bow.

Area E

A pecked rectangular figure, about six inches tall, created among a large number of animals and large Ghost Dance style birds. There are five pecked dots above the figure's head and four smaller ones at each side. A long legged animal appears near the figure's right hand.

Area E

Panel of humans and animals created by one artist. The arrangement of the subjects is in the biographical compositional style of painting on buffalo skin robes of the 1800's. A circular bodied figure on the left side of the photograph carries a spiral form.

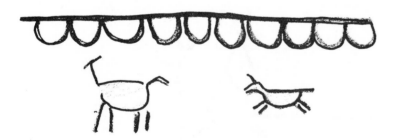

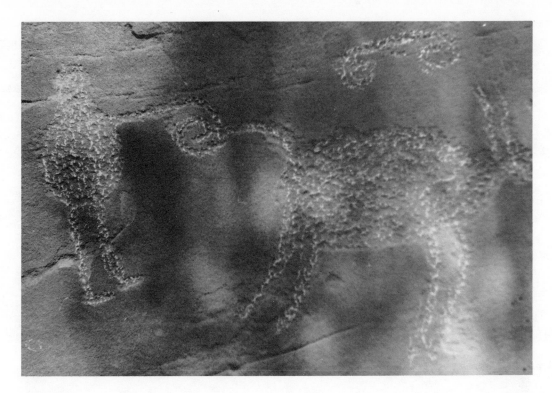

Area E

Closer view of the figure described in the preceding photo.

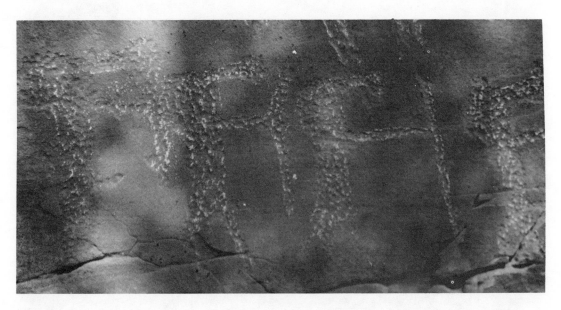

Area E

The Sun Dance or O-kee-pa ceremonies of some Plains tribes included humans dressed in buffalo hides with the heads attached. The four figures in profile on this panel may be buffalo dancers.

Area E

Ghost Dance style bird.

Area E

Ghost Dance style bird.

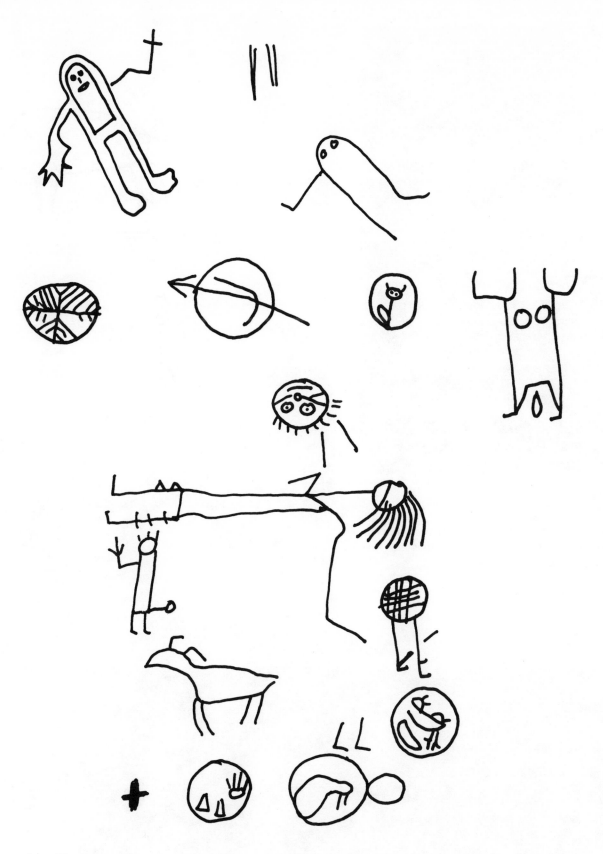

Area E

Drawing of depictions in northeastern Area E. The incised rectangular bodied figures are characteristic of Areas C, D, E, and F, Map #1. The composite circular designs are similar to those of Castle Gardens in central Wyoming, which were also applied to a surface prepared by abrading.

Area E

Composite design figure having a circular or "shield-bearing" body and a vertical rectangular body with a V-neck.

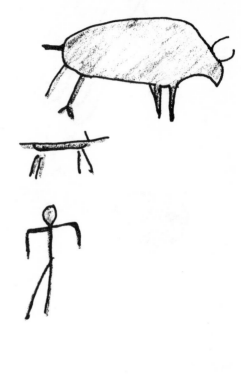

Area E

226

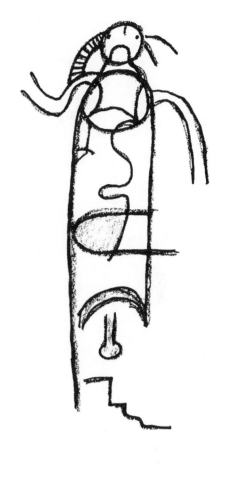

Area E

Panel of pecked art by one artist. Biographical style design. Animals, human-like figures and abstractions. Chalking has distorted the panel. Some depictions unchalked.

Area F

Area F

Lightly pecked figure with a disk on its breast.

Area F

A human-like figure on the same boulder as the preceding photo. The feet of this figure are turned with toes together. A large arrow crosses its lower body. The point of the arrow is on the right side of the photo.

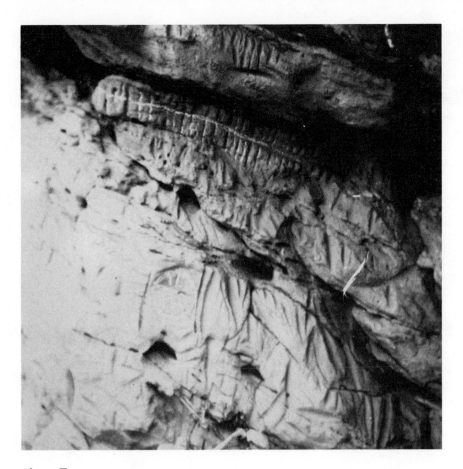

Area F

A cliff with a rough and broken surface which is nearly covered with slash or coups marks.

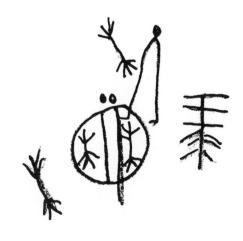

233

Area F

Composite circular style figure carrying a spear and an unidentified tool.

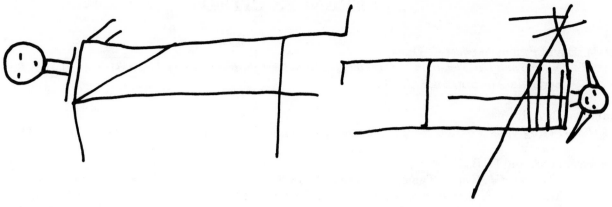

Area F

Drawing of two horizontal human-like figures with their feet toward each other. These figures are found at the site in Area F, which has numerous slash or coup marks.

REFERENCES CITED

Aberle, David F. and Stewart C. Omer
    1957   *Navajo and Ute Peyotism: A Chronological and Distributional Study.* University of Colorado Studies. Series in Anthropology No. 6.

Badhorse, Beverly
    1979   *Petroglyphs: Possible Religious Significance of Some.* Wyoming Archaeologist, Vol. XVIII, No. 2.

Cosgrove, H. S. and C. B.
    1932   *The Swart's Ruin, A Typical Mimbres Site In Southwestern New Mexico.* Papers of the Peabody Museum of American Archaeology and Ethnology, Harvard University, Vol. 15, XV, No. 1, Cambridge, Mass.

Drucker, Phillip
    1955   *Indians of the Northwest Coast.* McGraw-Hill Book Co., Inc., New York.

Ewers, John C.
    1939   *Plains Indian Painting. A Description of an Aboriginal American Art.* Stanford University Press. Stanford University, California. Humphrey Milford Oxford University Press, London.

    1967   *O-Kee-Pa: A Religioius Ceremony and other Customs of the Mandans.* By George Catlin with an Introduction by John C. Ewers. University Press. New Haven and London.

Fewkes, Jesse Walter
    1900   *Property Right In Eagles Among the Hopi.* American Anthropologist, N.S. 2.

Frison, George C.
    1978   *Prehistoric Hunters of the High Plains.* Academic Press, New York, San Francisco, London. A subsidiary of Harcourt-Brace Jovanovich, Publishers.

Galvan, Mary Elizabeth
    1977   *Vegetable Resources. A Cultural Resource Inventory of the Muddy Creek Divide and Lost Wells Butte Areas Near Riverton, Wyoming.* Edited by George M. Zeimens and Danny Walker. Publication of the Office of the State Archaeologist, Wyoming.

Gebhard, David S.,
    1969   *The Rock Art of Dinwoody, Wyoming.* An exhibition organized by David Gebhard. The Art Galleries, University of California. September 30 to November 6, 1969.

Hebard, Grace Raymond
    1930   *Washakie.* The Arthur H. Clark Co. Cleveland.

La Barre, Weston
    1964   *The Peyote Cult.* New Enlarged Edition. The Shoestring Press, Inc. Hamden, Connecticut. 1959-1964.

Larson, T. A.
    1965   *History of Wyoming.* University of Nebraska Press, Lincoln.

Mallery, Garrick
    1886   *Pictographs of the North American Indians: A Preliminary Paper,* Bureau of American Ethnology. 4th Annual Report 1882-83.

    1893   *Picture Writing of the American Indians.* Bureau of American Ethnology, 10th Annual Report, 1888-89.

Mooney, James
   1892   *A Kiowa Mescal Rattle.* American Anthropologist. Vol. V, January 1892.

   1896   *The Ghost Dance Religion and the Sioux Outbreak of 1890.* Fourteenth Annual Report of the Bureau of American Ethnology, 1892-93, Part 2. Washington, D.C.

Nicholson, Henry B.
   1971   *Religion in Pre-Hispanic Central Mexico.* Vol. 10, Handbook of the Middle American Indians. Robert Wauchope, General Editor. Published by the University of Texas Press, Ltd. London.

Putnam, J. D.
   1876   *Hieroglyphics Observed in Summit Canyon, Utah, and on Little Popo Agie River in Wyoming.* Proceedings of Davenport Academy of Natural Sciences, 1867-1876. Vol. 1.

Reher, Charles A.
   1977   *A Cultural Inventory of the Muddy Ridge Divide and Lost Wells Butte Area Near Riverton, Wyoming.* Publication of the Office of the State Archaeologist, Wyoming. Edited by George Zeimens and Danny Walker.

Reher, Charles A., and George C. Frison
   1980   *The Vore Site, 48CK302, A Stratified Buffalo Jump in the Wyoming Black Hills.* Plains Anthropologist, Vol. 25, No. 88, Part 2, May 1980. Memoir 16.

Renaud, E. B.
   1936   *Pictographs and Petroglyphs of the High Western Plains.* Archaeological Survey of the High Western Plains, 8th Annual Report. Department of Anthropology, University of Denver.

Slotkin, J. S.
   1956   *The Peyote Religion.* University of Chicago, The Free Press, Glencoe, Illinois.

Sowers, Ted C.
   1939   *Eight Sites.* Archaeological Project. Work Projects Administration.

   1940   *Petroglyphs and Pictographs of Dinwoody.* Archaeological Project. Work Projects Administration. Unpublished report, Natrona County Public Library, Casper.

Stenberg, M. P.
   1946   *The Peyote Cult Among Wyoming Indians.* University of Wyoming Publications, 12.

Trenholm, Virginia Cole and Maurine Carley
   1964   *The Shoshonis: Sentinels of the Rockies.* University of Oklahoma Press. Norman.

Wedel, Waldo R.
   1961   *Prehistoric Man On The Great Plains.* University of Oklahoma Press. Norman.

Willey, Gordon R.
   1966   *An Introduction to American Archaeology, North and Middle America,* Vol. 1. Prentice-Hall, Inc. Englewood Cliffs, N. J.

Zeimens, George and Danny Walker, et al.
   1977   *Inventory of the Muddy Ridge Divide and Lost Wells Butte Area Near Riverton, Wyoming.* Publication of the Office of the State Archaeologist, Wyoming.

REFERENCES FOR ROCK ART STUDIES AND
RELATED RESEARCH NOT CITED

Bozovich, Joseph and Joseph F.
  1968   *The White Mountain Petroglyphs.* Wyoming Archaeologist. Vol. 11, No. 2, July 1968.

Cain, H. T.
  1950   *Petroglyphs of Central Washington.* University of Washington Press. Seattle.

Carbonne, Gerald
  1972   *An Amateur's General Surface Report of the Tongue River Area.* Wyoming Archaeologist, Vol. XV, No. 4, December 1972.

Connor, Stuart and Betty Lou
  1971   *Rock Art of the Montana High Plains.* Exhibition for the Art Galleries, University of California. Santa Barbara.

Cressman, L. S.
  1937   *Petroglyphs of Oregon.* University of Oregon. Studies in Anthropology. No. 2, Eugene.

Day, Kent C., and David S. Dibble
  1963   *Archaeological Survey of the Flaming Gorge Reservoir Area, Wyoming, Utah.* University of Utah Anthropological Papers, No. 65. (Upper Colorado Series, No. 9)

Dorsey, James Owen
  1894   *A Study of Siouan Cults.* Bureau of American Ethnology. 11th Annual Report. Washington, D.C.

Erwin, R. P.
  1930   *Rock Writing In Idaho.* Idaho Historical Society, Biennial Report, No. 12. Boise, 1929-30.

Fewkes, Jesse Walter
  1898   *Expedition to Arizona, 1895.* Bureau of American Ethnology, 17th Annual Report, 1895-96. Washington, D.C.

Grant, Campbell
  1967   *Rock Art of the American Indian,* Thomas Y. Crowell Co., New York.

  1978   *Canyon De Chelly, Its People and Rock Art.* University of Arizona Press. Tucson.

Guernsey, Samuel J. and Alfred V. Kidder
  1921   *Northeastern Arizona: Report of the Explorations of 1916-17.* Papers of the Peabody Museum of American Archaeology and Ethnology, 8, (2). Cambridge.

Harrington, M. R.
  1928   *Tracing the Pueblo Boundary in Nevada.* Museum of the American Indian, Heye Foundation. Indian Notes, 5.

Haury, Emil W.
  1945   *Painted Cave, Northeastern Arizona.* The Amerind Foundation, Inc. Publications No. 3 Dragoon, Arizona.

Heizer, Robert F. and Martin Baumhoff
  1962   *Prehistoric Art of Nevada and Eastern California.* University of California Press.

Hinthorn, Juanita
  1962   *Turner Ranch Pictographs.* Wyoming Archaeologist. Vol. 5, No. 4. December, 1962.

Kirkland, Forrest and W. W. Newcomb
   1967   *The Rock Art of Texas Indians.* University of Texas Press: Austin and London.

Kroeber, A. L.
   1902   *The Arapaho.* Bulletins of the American Museum of Natural History. Vol. XVIII, New York.

   1925   *Handbook of the Indians of California.* Bureau of American Ethnology. Bulletin, No. 78.

Malloy, William
   1958   *Pictograph Cave, A Preliminary Historical Outline for the Northwestern Plains.* University of Wyoming. Vol. 22, No. 1.

Malouf, Carling
   1961   *Pictographs and Petroglyphs.* Archaeology In Montana. Vol 3, No. 1, Montana Archaeological Society, Missoula, Montana.

Mindeleff, Cosmos
   1897   *Cliff Ruins of Canyon de Chelly, Arizona.* 16th Annual Report of the Bureau of American Ethnology. Washington, D. C., 1894-95.

Over, W. H.
   1941   *Indian Picture Writing in South Dakota.* University of South Dakota Museum. Circular IV, Vermillion, South Dakota.

Renaud, E. B.
   1932   *Archaeological Survey of Eastern Wyoming.* Department of Anthropology, University of Denver, Denver, Colorado.

Secrist, K. G.
   1960   *Pictographs in Central Montana.* Anthropology and Sociology Papers, No. 20. University of Montana. Missoula.

Schaafsma, Polly
   1963   *Rock Art in the Navajo Reservoir District.* Papers in Anthropology, No. 7. Museum of New Mexico. Santa Fe.

   1971   *The Rock Art of Utah.* From the Donald Scott Collection. Papers of the Peabody Museum of Archaeology and Ethnology. Vol. 65. Harvard University, Cambridge.

   1972   *Rock Art In New Mexico.* State Planning Office. Santa Fe, New Mexico.

Sowers, Ted C.
   1941   *The Wyoming Archaeological Survey.* Federal Works Project Administration, State of Wyoming. University of Wyoming.

Steward, Julian H.
   1937   *Petroglyphs of the United States.* Smithsonian Report for 1936.

Strong, W. D., W. E. Schenck, and Julian H. Steward
   1930-32 *Petroglyphs of the Dalles-Deschutes Region.* American Archaeology and Ethnology. Vol. XXIX.

Tatum, R. M.
   1946   *Distribution and Bibliography of the Petroglyphs of the United States.* American Antiquity, 12.

Winger, G. R.
   1956   *The Pictographs and Petroglyphs Sites in an Archaeological Survey of Southern Blue Mountain and Douglas Creek in Northwestern Colorado.* Master of Art Thesis, Denver University. Denver.

Wormington, H. M.
   1955   *A Reappraisal of the Fremont Culture.* Denver Museum of Natural History. Proceedings No. 1.